The Earth
and
the Fullness Thereof

The Earth
and
the Fullness Thereof

A Down-Home Reader in Ecological Theology

H. PAUL SANTMIRE

CASCADE *Books* • Eugene, Oregon

THE EARTH AND THE FULLNESS THEREOF
A Down-Home Reader in Ecological Theology

Copyright © 2024 H. Paul Santmire. All rights reserved. Except for brief quotations in critical publications or reviews, no part of this book may be reproduced in any manner without prior written permission from the publisher. Write: Permissions, Wipf and Stock Publishers, 199 W. 8th Ave., Suite 3, Eugene, OR 97401.

Cascade Books
An Imprint of Wipf and Stock Publishers
199 W. 8th Ave., Suite 3
Eugene, OR 97401

www.wipfandstock.com

PAPERBACK ISBN: 979-8-3852-1348-1
HARDCOVER ISBN: 979-8-3852-1349-8
EBOOK ISBN: 979-8-3852-1350-4

Cataloguing-in-Publication data:

Names: Santmire, H. Paul, author.

Title: The earth and the fullness thereof : a down-home reader in ecological theology / H. Paul Santmire.

Description: Eugene, OR: Cascade Books, 2024. | Includes bibliographical references.

Identifiers: ISBN 979-8-3852-1348-1 (paperback). | ISBN 979-8-3852-1349-8 (hardcover). | ISBN 979-8-3852-1350-4 (epub).

Subjects: LSCH: Ecotheology. | Nature—Religious aspects—Christianity. | Creation. | Human ecology—Religious aspects—Christianity.

Classification: BT695.5 S25 2024 (print). | BT695.5 (epub).

Scripture quotations marked (NRSV) are from the New Revised Standard Version Bible, copyright © 1989 the Division of Christian Education of the National Council of the Churches of Christ in the United States of America. Used by permission. All rights reserved.

Scripture quotations marked (RSV) are taken from Revised Standard Version of the Bible, copyright © 1946, 1952, and 1971 National Council of the Churches of Christ in the United States of America. Used by permission. All rights reserved worldwide.

Scripture quotations marked (KJV) are taken from The Authorized (King James) Version. Rights in the Authorized Version in the United Kingdom are vested in the Crown. Reproduced by permission of the Crown's patentee, Cambridge University Press

To David Gagne

Contents

Preface: A Down-Home Reader? | ix

Part One: **Where I'm Coming From**
I   Why Should Anyone Listen to An Old White Guy? | 3
II   Earth Day Fifty: Insights in the Rearview Mirror | 8
III   What I Told My College Classmates Sixty Years Later | 13

Part Two: **Current Issues**
IV   Breaking Down Our Moral Breakdown | 21
V   Celebrating City, Farm, and Wilderness Together: An Un-American Theology for Nature's Nation? | 26
VI   What's the Best Way to Shrink Your Carbon Footprint? | 36
VII How to Be a Christian Citizen in These Times of Crisis | 41

Part Three: **Spiritual Explorations**
VIII The Avocado and the Onion: Two Spiritualities | 49
IX   Cutting Through the Ice to Encounter the Depths | 54
X   Natural Images for Contemplating the Trinity | 60
XI   Praying All the Time? Practicing the Trinity Prayer Inside and Outside | 66
XII On the Habit of Noticing: A Report from the Big Island | 75

Part Four: **Living Ecologically**

XIII Gardening as Resistance | 87

XIV Caring for Creation Isn't Enough | 91

XV From Lake Wobegon to the Streets of Manhattan | 95

Part Five: **Testimony from the Arts**

XVI Gnosticism and the Earthly Vision of Vincent Van Gogh | 101

XVII J. M. W. Turner's Slave Ship, Nature, and Having Eyes to See | 108

XVIII Titian: Women, Myth, Power—and Nature | 112

Part Six: **Faith's Cosmic Vision** | 117

XIX Who Then Is This? From "Jesus Loves Me" to "the Cosmic Christ" | 119

Other Books by the Author | 130

Preface
A Down-Home Reader?

THIS IS A DIFFERENT kind of book, not due to its unifying biblical theme, the earth and the fullness thereof, which has long preoccupied me and which, these days, thankfully, is a familiar topic in many church educational and activist discussions. Rather, this a different kind of book because of what it's not.

Here I'm *not* asking you, the reader of this Reader, to follow a single argument, chapter by chapter, to its conclusion. Rather, I'm inviting you to reflect about a number of apparently disparate themes in ecological theology that I believe hold together, but only retrospectively. They're down-home themes for me, moreover, because they're so deeply personal: (I) Where I'm Coming From, (II) Current Issues, (III) Spiritual Explorations, (IV) Living Ecologically, (V) Testimony from the Arts, and (VI) Faith's Cosmic Vision.

That being said, I hope that it will be apparent at every turn that I have long understood the construct ecological theology broadly. By it I mean much more than what has sometimes been called the theology of nature. Ecological theology, for me, isn't just about God and nature. It's also about God and us humans and our relationships with one another and with nature and about anything that throws light on those relationships.

And more. Ecological theology, for me, is about all the aforementioned—*in a time of crisis*. Each of my books, this one included, has taken that urgent global fact for granted. But the critical question for me always has been, and still is, this: confronted by our world's momentous and increasingly severe ecojustice predicament, is there a viable faith-driven way to live realistically and hopefully and engagedly on God's good Earth today?

My response in this book, as in all my previous writings, is an enthusiastic Yes. But this book differs from most of my works, because, as I've already indicated, it's a cover-to-cover narrative of my own experience, as I have responded to a broad range of eco-theological and related existential challenges for many years. This book is down-home in that intensely personal sense.

Down-home also means, for me, that I am primarily addressing a particular group of readers. While I will surely welcome the company of professional theologians, my purpose here is to engage parish pastors, congregational lay leaders, and spiritual seekers more generally. In the good old days, true, some of us used to refer to those whom I am including in my target audience as "the regulars": the pastors, the people in the pews, and the visitors. Great idea, but not totally accurate anymore.

These days, those from younger generations in particular may not be in the pews so much, either as members or as visitors, even though, I surmise, more than a few of them are at least in some moments eager to become what might be called deep Christians. So, emphatically, this book is not just for "the regulars," critically important as they are for the life of the church. All the more so, it's for those who have stationed themselves at the periphery of the church's life. In our time, these folks are sometimes called "seekers." And I'm eager to speak with them here, wherever they might be hanging out, near a church or somewhere else.

My hope, then, is that all readers of this Reader, church members, younger and older, clergy and laity, *and* seekers of any age or station in life, might benefit from encounters with the insights that I will be exploring here: so that all can ponder what it might mean to walk the Christian way more confidently and more joyfully, as all of us continue to respond to the sometimes frightening, frequently confusing, and often depressing ecological and spiritual challenges of these times of global crisis.

Preface

Most of the chapters in this Reader have already appeared in print or online in some form, but I have thoroughly revised them for publication here. For readers who would like to check out my other books, I have provided a list at the end of this volume.

The Earth and the Fullness Thereof is dedicated to a beloved and long-standing friend of mine, David Gagne, who currently lives in Minneapolis. Trained once in Belgium as a candidate for the Catholic priesthood, David eventually decided to find a much more public and prophetic ministry of his own in the US, beyond the institutional church, above all through his energetic and imaginative peace witness over many decades. He has long encouraged me by his prophetic vision, by his deep piety, by his inspired social activism, by his collaborative style, and by his personal kindnesses.

H. Paul Santmire

Easter 2024

PART ONE

Where I'm Coming From

I

Why Should Anyone Listen to an Old White Guy?

THIS IS A QUESTION I've thought about a lot lately, because I've recently been reminded, by my daughter and by one of her two daughters, that it's much on the mind of younger generations these days. While those two key women in my own life, I have observed, do try to listen to me with a spirit of generosity, I have every reason to ponder their take on folks like me more generally. What good can come from the likes of me? Three strikes and I'm out, right? Old. White. Guy. Straight, too, I hasten to add. So: four strikes.

I.

I *have* found myself in this kind of predicament before. And I survived. That's somehow reassuring. Beginning in 1968, for reasons that I never fully understood at the time, I found myself serving as the chaplain—yes, a *male* chaplain—of Wellesley College, an all-women's institution in New England. That institution was not only peopled by women; it was run by women for women, eagerly.

On numerous occasions, I would find myself in a room full of what was then sometimes thought of as "the second sex"—various gatherings of students, faculty, and staff—with me being the only male present. They would just chatter on, sometimes with two or three speaking at the same time, occasionally discussing the telltale ways of men, as if I weren't in the room!

More by necessity than by wisdom, I soon learned that the best place for me to be during such meetings was in the back of the room; and the best thing for me to do there would be to keep my mouth shut. Even if I thought I had something to say! Sure, speak when spoken to. But that was it.

Thirteen years later, with Wellesley College then behind me, I found myself as the pastor of a small, inner-city congregation in what was then the fourth poorest city in the US, Hartford, Connecticut. My understanding in accepting a call to that church—affirmed by its leaders—was that I was to aspire to be a pastor for the whole neighborhood, however the Spirit might lead me to do that, not just the pastor of that mostly white, middle-class congregation.

Soon I started visiting residents in that neighborhood. Many of them, it turned out, were low-income Black women, often living on welfare. In due course, I also found myself head-over-heels involved in fostering a community organization, inspired by the confrontational methods of the great Saul Alinsky.

In that process, sparked on by the energies and the vision of a young white Irish Catholic guy, a trained community organizer with an attitude, I sometimes would find myself sitting in a living room jammed full of welfare mothers, as I thought of them in those days—African Americans, most of them, who were by and large unknown in the white, middle-class world that I knew best. That organizer would ask them, emphatically: what did *they* want to see happen in *their* neighborhood?

Then, typically, the room would erupt in intense conversations, almost, again, as had happened to me at Wellesley, as if he and I were not in the room. When the white power structure in Hartford and its suburbs came up in those discussions, those women would roll their eyes in knowing ways that would make me want to go hide behind a curtain. Back at Wellesley, I kept my mouth shut in group meetings, because I didn't really know how to get a word in edgewise. There, in Hartford, I kept my mouth shut, because I had nothing to say. Sure, I would, once again, speak when spoken to. But, again, that was that.

In retrospect, I think that that pattern of default wisdom served me well both at Wellesley and in Hartford. Speak when spoken to. Otherwise, sit quietly in the back of the room. Often, I should add, both at Wellesley and in Hartford, I was asked to speak at the *beginning* of meetings, but that was to pray. Even so, speaking to God publicly in such situations was a frightful business for me back then (and still is), so I kept my prayers short and to the point. Then I would sit down in the last row and listen.

Or, stand up and go with them. That was an invitation that kept coming my way both at Wellesley College and in Hartford. Student activists—like Hillary Rodham (later Clinton)—wanted me to go with them when they met with the college president to demand that Wellesley recruit more Black students. Welfare mothers in Hartford wanted me to go with them when they stormed into a meeting at city hall, demanding to be heard. At such times, I often felt like a fifth wheel. But I also felt blessed to be there.

II.

Which brings me to my most recent book, *EcoActivist Testament: Faith Explorations for Fellow Travelers*. As an old white guy, I am indeed something of a fifth wheel. But, as I've said, I feel blessed—unashamedly waiting in the back of the room, but now, also unashamedly pushing that book, which may be my most important publication—precisely because it's about doing stuff. The title sounds ambitious, but what I thought about all the time when I was writing it was this: this book's for you, whichever generation-after-me you're a part of, *just in case you might ask*.

And more. Both at Wellesley and in Hartford, I did a lot of what was called in those days pastoral counseling, mostly with women. But, in retrospect, that enterprise was mainly pastoral listening. When those mostly affluent young women at Wellesley College and those low-income African American mothers spoke to me one-on-one, whether in my office or in inner-city pizza parlors, I almost always stood in awe of them. Early on and then consistently thereafter, I learned that the phrases "a strong woman" and, all the more so, "a strong Black woman" are more often than not redundant.

No surprise, then: as I've been noting about times when I attended group or public meetings, only rarely would *I* speak in one-to-one personal counseling sessions. Occasionally, to be sure, one of those women would ask me, "And what do you think?" Then, as in public settings, I would tell them, briefly.

I feel the same way about *EcoActivist Testament*. Yes, I wrote that little book for new generations of Christian ecoactivists, whose amazing commitments and whose strong and often, to me, complex ways of engaging issues I may only dimly understand. But I wrote that book from the back of the room, as it were—as an old, white, and straight guy who's been working with these ecoactivist issues since before the first Earth Day—just in case somebody might ask me, "And what do you think?"

More particularly, in recent years, I've been trying to give the message of *EcoActivist Testament* legs, as it were, by being as supportive as I can of an extraordinary grassroots church movement, run by energetic and visionary ecoactivists, most of them much younger than I, all of them deeply committed to the struggle for global ecojustice. As Lutherans Restoring Creation (LRC) thankfully continues to flourish, I'm delighted to hang out, now and again, with some LRC activists, mostly these days via Zoom—not primarily to speak, but mainly to listen as best as I can.

I am heartened, too, that LRC is by no means the only organization of its kind in the US today. *Virtually all American Christian denominations now have ecojustice movements of their own, mostly driven by younger activists.* Praise the Lord for that.

Shouldn't all Christians in the American ecumenical world enthusiastically support such grassroots church initiatives? Of course. Especially we older white males—above all, by digging deeply into our pockets. Financial support for groups like LRC, indeed, might be the most important thing that someone like me can give in these times of global crisis. In a word, first and foremost let my checkbook do the talking, along with other stuff perhaps, like writing books.

II

Earth Day Fifty
Insights in the Rearview Mirror

For me, April 22, 2020, was not just the celebration of the first Earth Day fifty years before, but it also was a more personal time for me to begin some ruminating. I published my first book in ecological theology the same year as the first Earth Day—*Brother Earth* (1970). In those days, mine was one of a very few voices addressing ecological and ecojustice issues theologically.

I invite you to join me now to see what we can see as we look back on those days. As anyone who has a driver's license can l tell you, sometimes looking in the rearview mirror can make a big difference about what your next move along the road is going to be.

I.

Brother Earth? I had to struggle even to come up with a title for that book. My first impulse had been to think in terms of "Mother Earth." But in those days many Christians—who were then, as now, my main audience—were highly suspicious of anything that sounded like "paganism" or "nature religion." Those were the days, too, when numerous American Christian thinkers were, following the great Swiss Reformed theologian, Karl Barth, zealously opposed anything that even sounded as if it might be some kind of "natural theology."

On the other hand, American Christians—especially American Protestants!—had never wavered in their adulation for that great medieval Catholic saint Francis of Assisi. And, privately but zealously, I wanted to claim Francis as my own patron saint, since I was seeking to identify a new and compelling kind of Christian love for nature. Francis, as is well-known, had freely used familial language for nature. So, for me, *Brother Earth* it was.

To be sure, I would later come to publicly express some regret for that choice. Why? The year 1970 also marked, for me, the beginning of a new kind of vocational adventure, to which I have already alluded. I had just begun my ministry as Wellesley College's first chaplain. There, I soon realized that if I were to survive, never mind to thrive, in that women's world as a male ecological theologian, I would have to become a champion of a new form of Christian theology that was emerging in those days, ecofeminism.

Hence, I invited Mary Daly, author of the then notorious—for many people who cared about such things at that time—*Beyond God the Father* (1973), to speak in the college chapel. She would be the first of many other ecofeminist preachers whom I would bring to Wellesley. And, in due course, I began to teach a course in ecological theology, the first of its kind in the college's history, highlighting the works of ecofeminist thinkers like Daly and Rosemary Radford Ruether.

In retrospect—so I came to believe in ensuing years—I could well have titled my first book *Mother Earth* or even *Sister Earth*. But publishing, like politics, has always been the art of the possible. Given the patriarchal propensities of American church life in the early 1970s, I probably had done very well, I finally concluded, with the title *Brother Earth*. At least that had been a step in the right direction.

II.

Following the publication of *Brother Earth*, although I didn't abandon other personal and professional commitments, I nevertheless devoted myself to ecological theology and ecojustice activism, which some colleagues considered a fetish or even a fixation. It has surely been a lifelong passion for me since the 1960s, predicated on an increasingly urgent anxiety. Not for nothing did the word "crisis" appear in the title of many of my books, beginning with my first, fully titled: *Brother Earth: Nature, God, and Ecology in a Time of Crisis*.

On April 22, 2020, however, when I was reflecting about the previous fifty years, I was in fact sheltering in place, a good thing for an octogenarian like me to have been doing in that era of the coronavirus pandemic. In my view at that time, that enormous scourge might well have been just the first wave of a number of global disasters that were about to afflict God's good earth in the decades that were to come, and especially the poor.

As a lifelong follower of the Christian way, I of course wanted to have hope, theologically. And I did—and still do. But I was not existentially optimistic back then, nor am I now. Still, I stood then, as I stand now, with Martin Luther, who—reportedly—when he was once was asked what he would do if the world were about to come to an end, was said to have offered these, by now oft-quoted, words, "I would plant an apple tree."

Which I take to mean: whatever else all of us might be called upon to do in this era of global crisis—who knows what horrific challenges may await humans during the *next* fifty years—we all should do the good and seek the justice that each of us has been called upon to do and to seek, with passion, wisdom, and without ceasing.

For me, much of my time over the previous fifty years had been given to cultivating the field of ecological theology. To be sure, I'm aware that much if not all of those labors were parochial in the strict sense of that word—and still are. I acted and wrote self-consciously and publicly as a card-carrying Christian and as a Lutheran Christian in particular, who aspired to be a public, ecumenical theologian. Many of my writings are now relatively well-known in US Christian circles, and at least a couple of them, such as *The Travail of Nature*, are publicly well regarded. Lesser known, but to me perhaps my most important theological work, have been my efforts to influence the thought and practice of my own particular Christian communion, American Lutheranism.

III.

Why? I have long claimed the sentiments that I was taught by that Hartford community organizer, to whom I referred above, as a maxim: *grow where you are planted*. That field, for me, for better for worse, has been the life and faith of Lutheran traditions, understood as a reform movement within the holy catholic church.

Thus I had a hand in shaping major statements on the environment by the Lutheran Church in America (1972) and the Evangelical Lutheran Church in America (1993), and I continue to serve as a consultant for the sometimes struggling but visionary grassroots movement Lutherans Restoring Creation, to which I have already referred.

As an ecumenically oriented Lutheran, I wrote my most recent book, *EcoActivist Testament*, in the wake of Pope Francis's amazing encyclical, *Laudato si'*.[1] My work invites readers, especially those who identify with the Christian tradition—if I may put it this way—to get with it for the sake of Jesus.

Further, I wrote *Brother Earth*, now more than fifty years ago, in part to respond to the then increasingly—and still, in some circles—popular 1966 claim of the historian Lynn White Jr. that Christianity as a faith tradition had been, for the most part, ecologically bankrupt (!). I there argued, and in many other writings as well, that White's thesis was an important *half-truth*. Yes, we must be well aware of how Christianity has been complicit over

---

1. Pope Francis, *Laudato si'*, encyclical letter, May 24, 2015, https://www.vatican.va/content/dam/francesco/pdf/encyclicals/documents/papa-francesco_20150524_enciclica-laudato-si_en.pdf/.

the centuries in cultural trends that have led to the abuse and the degradation of nature and of the poor of the earth.

But that's not the whole story, by any means. Historic Christianity has also championed a second—ecological!—tradition. Hence my chief vocation as one who has aspired to be a public theologian of the holy catholic church: to identify, to reformulate, and then to champion that rich ecological tradition of Christian life and thought, which has now been brought to a kind of historic fulfilment in Pope Francis's *Laudato Si'*.[2]

IV.

As of April 22, 2020, then, when I was sheltering at home, I was grateful that I had been given my long-standing vocation to serve as an ecological theologian rooted in Lutheran traditions, among a then emerging global ecumenical community of theologians and practitioners, led by Pope Francis, all of whom are committed to the life and the mission of the holy catholic church and, in particular, to its ecological and ecojustice witness in this, our apocalyptic era.

---

2. Pope Francis, *Laudato si'*.

III

What I Told My College Classmates Sixty Years Later

I SUSPECT THAT MOST members of the class of 1957 will not want that "ancient Chinese curse," which I once learned on the streets when I was doing community organizing, to come true: "may you live in interesting times." In that spirit, I will only briefly narrate a few family matters here. Then I will get to the single thing that's been preoccupying me for decades, which I believe is really interesting.

I.

My wife, Laurel, and I live in Watertown, a mile away from Harvard Square, a distance that I used to walk regularly, after we moved to this small city, some two decades ago, upon my retirement. I don't do that walking anymore, however, not primarily because of COVID-19 restrictions or anything like that, but because of my own arthritic knees. My contact with the old school these days, for a variety of reasons, is mainly at a distance.

A few years ago, for sure, I was able to find a way to yell at the university to get rid of its holdings in fossil fuel stocks and that was gratifying. I joined a sizeable crowd of students, faculty, staff, and alumnae/i, including Harvard grad Bill McKibben, to raise a prophetic ruckus in front of University Hall. "Divest!" we all cried out.

In another context, on the home front, I decided early on after graduation, and have continued to believe with enthusiasm ever since, that the traditional language of the church is right: marriage *is* a "holy estate," notwithstanding its all too frequent existential anguish. Laurel and I have been married, blessedly, for more than fifty years. Not too long ago, I even wrote a scholarly autobiographical essay about "marital spirituality," celebrating this holy estate—for better, for worse; for richer, for poorer; in sickness and in health.

Our two children and their families live relatively near us, our son, Matthew, in suburban Wayland, Massachusetts, where he's a special-education teacher and our daughter, Heather, in Portland, Maine, where she shepherds her own grant-writing business, aimed to serve nonprofit groups and agencies. We see our children and their families often, especially when they visit us at our home-away-from-home in rural southwestern Maine, a rooted place that I've written about frequently.

Turns out that I have now lived in retirement at my current Massachusetts address longer than I have ever lived anywhere else, more than two decades. During most of my adult life, in contrast, given my vocation as a student and then as a campus and parish pastor and as a teaching theologian over the years, I moved from setting to setting frequently.

Along the way, one of the professional endeavors that held my life together, was this. I ended up being a writer of sorts, producing a wheelbarrowful of articles and books, which has given my vocational trajectory a certain organic unity, notwithstanding my bumping around geographically to different assignments. I am grateful for all this, even though I never intended it to happen this way.

II.

That organic unity, in retrospect, began to come into view for me already when I was a doctoral student at Harvard Divinity School in the 1960s. Back then I helped to invent a new field, ecological theology, and I have been at it, in a variety of contexts, ever since, beginning with my first book, *Brother Earth*, in 1970. Since then I've published eight books in that now burgeoning field—a field that has been brought to its most important and most stunning expression thus far by Pope Francis's 2015 encyclical, *Laudato si'*.[1]

Which brings me to the longest chapter of my own vocational story, ecoactivism, which for me has been both profoundly fulfilling and profoundly troubling. Everything that I've stood for publicly for more than sixty years, I believe, now stands or falls with this commitment. As I've often observed, in profoundly sophisticated theological terms, our world is now going to hell. Not an original insight, I know. But if the truth be known, too many Christians, especially right-wing American Catholics and right-wing Evangelical Protestants, have mainly been preoccupied with other issues.

On the other hand, movements for ecosanity and ecojustice and ecohealing have arisen all around the globe in recent years, especially evident in the ranks of generations more recent than mine. Even Harvard is beginning to divest from fossil fuel investments, thanks to the persistence of mostly young activists. And numerous religious types, like me, have consistently, if not always visibly, been involved in such actions.

The question, as all who really think about these things will recognize, is this: will we humans, people of faith along with everyone else, be able to change our sinful ways in time? Probably not. For as Reinhold Niebuhr once observed, original sin, the only empirically demonstrable Christian teaching, is rampant in our midst.

---

1. Pope Francis, *Laudato si'*, encyclical letter, May 24, 2015, https://www.vatican.va/content/dam/francesco/pdf/encyclicals/documents/papa-francesco_20150524_enciclica-laudato-si_en.pdf/.

Once again, will the majority of Americans ever choose the common ecological good? Who knows? Not even God, I think.

But surely, for all of us who can read the signs of our apocalyptic times, the moment has arrived *to get with it*, wherever we might find ourselves today, drawing on whatever personal and political and financial resources we can muster. My father once said to me, gnomically, "when you take hold of the rug, you take hold of the whole rug." Whatever that might mean, it's obvious to me that everyone who cares about God's good earth must take hold of that earth somewhere, before it's too late.

III.

That's what I have tried to do, especially in this the last stage of my life, as a relatively rich old white guy, as one who's long been a de facto part of the global problematic of ecodestruction, socially and economically, as have many other Harvard graduates, some, who have had the most assets, probably more than others.

Here is a case in point. In recent years, I have done everything I can to support the ecojustice ministries of a grassroots church movement, Lutherans Restoring Creation (LRC). LRC is only one of several—usually underfunded—grassroots church ecojustice movements in the US and around the world. (I list some of them in chapter 1 of my book *EcoActivist Testament*).

LRC pushes advocacy for ecojustice at a national level and ecoeducation and calls for action at every level of my own faith community, the three-million-member Evangelical Lutheran Church in America (ELCA). LRC shepherds the creation of "green synods" and "green congregations" and "green lifestyles" in the ELCA and provides resources for ecojustice preaching and ecojustice renewal of congregations' liturgies and public witness. All this on a financial shoestring! Which sounds apostolic to me.

At my age, for sure, with my arthritic knees and my walking cane, I can't do too much street demonstrating anymore. (A couple of years ago, during a protest march against some Boston banks that lend to oil companies, the long line of participants walked so fast to the next bank that I, stationed at the very end, in order not to get in the way, got left behind! I just couldn't keep up.) I surely can't travel to stand for hours in snow-covered mud in the Midwest to support Indigenous activists, who are rising up against the latest fossil fuel pipeline in a winter protest, although, as I've indicated, I still can stand, at least for a time, in Harvard Yard and yell at Harvard, whenever that's necessary.

More generally, I can also raise holy hell with my voice whenever I can—interpersonally, in my voting, by my writing, and when I have a folding chair to sit on during public protests. And, perhaps most importantly, in consultation with my wife, I can find a way to invest some of our *assets*, not just our spare change, to help finance initiatives like LRC. You don't have to save the world, I keep telling myself, but you can take hold of the rug somewhere—and then hold on, for dear life, with hope.

PART TWO

Current Issues

IV

Breaking Down Our Moral Breakdown

REMEMBER THE GOOD OLD days when you didn't have to lock your doors? When kids could walk home from school all by themselves, go inside for a snack, and then just run outside to play all afternoon, and their parents didn't have to worry? Those were the days—or maybe not.

The celebrated Columbia University researcher, Adam M. Mastroianni, has argued, convincingly, that the good old days were in all likelihood not much better than our own days of—alleged—moral breakdown. [*Harvard Gazette*, June 15, 2023; *New York Times*, June 21, 2023]

I.

Some of us like to think otherwise. Some old folks, like me, seem to champion the life and values of the past, in contrast to the life and values of what we perceive to be our current Brave New World. Many of all ages, indeed, appear to believe that our American world is, as we speak, undergoing a serious moral breakdown.

That's because, Mastroianni argues, many of us tend to forget or repress painful memories from the past and to cherish the good memories from that selfsame past. Hence we are inclined to assume that current generations are undergoing a moral breakdown. To the contrary, Mastroianni argues, things today are pretty much the way they were generations ago, morally speaking. We're not experiencing a moral breakdown in our time; we're living with our own selective memories. The *New York Times* summarized Mastroisanni's findings this way: "Our biased attention means we'll always feel we're living in dark times, and our biased memory means we'll always think the past was brighter."

II.

I don't begrudge Mastroisanni his study. I welcome it. It feels true to me. The golden olden days were never as golden as some of us sometimes imagine them to have been. And, as Mastroianni stresses, it's critically important for these facts to be widely known, so that demagogues today won't find it so easy to promise us that *they* will take us back to some golden moral age, to "the real America" of the past.

But it appears to me that Mastroianni's project also tends to beg a huge question. It suggests, if it doesn't say so in so many words, that morality mainly pertains to *the acts of individuals*, whether today or in times gone by. Really?

Almost a century ago, the great American theologian and ethicist Reinhold Niebuhr tried to instruct all his fellow citizens that moral or immoral acts by individuals are only part of the story of our national ethos. Especially in his classic study, *Moral Man and Immoral Society*, Niebuhr argued, in effect, that the whole is greater than the sum of the parts. For Niebuhr, *collectives*—labor unions, political parties, the capitalist classes, business conglomerates, the nation-state, the military-industrial complex, and even some religious institutions—have huge, often inordinate power in our history. And often, not for the good. They frequently function as multipliers of individual greed and lust for power—a phenomenon, I believe, that was long ago portrayed by the New Testament's vision of the global, even cosmic, works of "the principalities and powers" of death and destruction (see Ephesians 4:12).

III.

Theologian Paul Tillich—for some years a colleague of Niebuhr—thought along the same lines when he projected his now frequently underplayed, even forgotten, theme about the world-historical and, indeed, the cosmic workings of what Tillich called "the Demonic." Tillich meant a number of things by that construct. But he surely had in mind the colossal destructivity of the German nation in the last century and that nation's Holocaust in particular. (Tillich himself had had to flee from Germany to the US when the Nazis were coming to power.)

How could a whole nation of, mostly, morally well-intentioned individuals, many of them devout Lutherans and devout Roman Catholics, many of whom treasured, above all, loving one's neighbor as oneself, become captive to the heinous forces of mass death unleashed by the Nazis, and choose not to impede, often not even to notice, the murder of six million Jews? In a sense, it was *the collectives* that did it: huge political, economic, and psychospiritual conglomerates overran a whole nation, sometimes by default, although all too often by intention, and, in so doing, virtually destroyed a whole people, the Jews.

Tillich thought of such collectives and their destructive ways as expressions of *the Demonic*. Tillich never tried to explain the origins or the workings of the Demonic in human and cosmic history. But he kept talking about it insistently, even though he knew that that was not a construct that would—in optimistic, individualizing America—help him to win friends and influence people. In doing this, Tillich gave voice to one of the oft-forgotten teachings of the great German Enlightenment philosopher Immanuel Kant—which ran so profoundly contrary to the optimism and the rationalism of Kant's own period. Kant insisted on the reality of what he called "radical evil."

Part Two: Current Issues

IV.

While it can be helpful, then, to ponder the moral breakdown of contemporary life in the US in terms of individual behavior and even to compare that breakdown to similar patterns in the past, that's not enough. That's only part of the story.

Here's a current example. Aren't many of us white Americans prisoners of the principalities and powers of racism? Whether or not we consciously espouse racist thoughts or practices? Sure, conversations about reparations have recently begun to emerge in our midst. But more often than not, by my observation, even those who engage in these often faltering conversations are talking the talk rather than walking the walk. Who can convincingly argue, in particular, that white American churches in our time are generally no longer captive to the Demonic in this respect, as so many of them have so egregiously been in the past?

Which has wrenching implications, it seems to me, for how we are to think about the ongoing ministries of predominantly white churches in the US. Should the primary moral goal of such congregations be to shape individuals to be good citizens? Or should the primary moral goal of such congregations be *to confront the Demonic*—to actively resist the Principalities and Powers of Death?

If it's the latter, as I believe it must be in our times, if we are to be found faithful to our calling to take up our crosses to follow Jesus, we white Christians are in for a struggle of colossal proportions. Sunday morning worship in particular, in addition to everything else that it must be, can no longer be just a process mostly aimed at supporting and enhancing the moral and spiritual growth of individual Christians. Our liturgy must not just be a school for souls, but somehow must become a *meeting to mobilize* our congregations for the struggle to which God has called us all.

Then there's spirituality, which is immensely popular these days. I'm not against it, by any means. I've written a book about it. But maybe what all of us who are struggling to be Christians today should be working on, first and foremost, is not spirituality as such, but the challenge to follow Jesus—which so overwhelmed Dietrich Bonhoeffer that he decided to participate in the plot to assassinate Hitler. Maybe most members of every predominantly white American congregation in these apocalyptic times should be reading Bonhoeffer's tract *The Cost of Discipleship* all over again.

Here is a sobering thought in this respect. How much are all of us in the US today, including many church members, *already* in the midst of a deadly protofascist period, like the Weimar era in Germany, in which Bonhoeffer lived as a young man? Is there a Hitler already in our midst and possibly also in our future? And, if so, what are we Christians doing in response to that prospect right now?

V.

The challenge for many of our churches today, it therefore appears to me, is by no means just to promote individual morality, nor just to nourish individual spirituality, but all the more so to struggle together against the Demonic. That, I believe, is how we should best break down our moral breakdown in these times.

V

Celebrating City, Farm, and Wilderness Together

An Un-American Theology for Nature's Nation?

THE EMINENT TWENTIETH-CENTURY AMERICAN historian Perry Miller once published a study in American history entitled *Nature's Nation*. Woody Guthrie gave expression to that theme in his own memorable way: "This land is your land . . . this land is my land . . . From the redwood forest to the Gulf Stream waters . . ." One of the nation's most celebrated authors, Henry David Thoreau, wrote extensively and intensively about the same motif: a life immersed in what he thought of as nature. Just about anyone who has studied American cultural history from colonial times on will also know the names of many other US writers of stature or celebrated artists or renowned activists or popularizing scientists who were likewise preoccupied with nature.

While Indigenous peoples have lived in and with nature on the North American continent for many centuries, and while countless thousands of Africans were once shipped here in chains to work the land, European colonists and their descendants, like me, have nevertheless made the very idea of nature our own, as Guthrie was wont to sing: "this land is my land." In this sense,

America, as colonized (and often as romanticized), has become nature's nation.

But which "nature" does this cultural construct in fact identify? How to define that venerable word? Those who have thought about this question have regularly been unable to come up with a rendering that's commensurate with the word's rich and often confusing meanings, whether in common or literary or scientific or theological usage. The noted American philosopher Arthur Lovejoy once identified dozens of meanings of the word nature. But sometimes define a term we must.

In our situation, I think, as long as we are aware of the ambiguities, it's intellectually permissible to think of nature as what we commonly call "the material world." Which is not all that different from what Christianity's Nicene Creed calls "all things visible."

I.

That being said, over the years, pursuant to my own interests in the theology of nature and, more particularly, the theology of ecojustice, I have chosen to move on from that definitional challenge—or morass—as quickly as possible into the world of biblical thought. This, in part, to respond critically to what I have perceived to be a certain problematic insularity in Euro-American life and thought concerning nature.

City-dwellers, for example, may well be indifferent to the needs of farmers. Or champions of rural America or of the wilderness may well advocate, politically, against public investments in the city. Cattle farmers may resent the idea of wilderness preservation when they have to deal with the attacks of wolves, say. Lovers of the wilderness may fight against a planned pipeline through a forest preserve, even though that project might benefit more than a few who live in cities, lower-income citizens in particular.

Justice is best served, it appears to me, by what might be called a holistic vision of nature—the material world—that presupposes *the equal importance of city, farm, and wilderness for American life today*. And it is good to know that such a holistic vision is available—in the Scriptures.

II.

The Bible, I believe, and as I now will try to show, offers us what might be called a trinitarian understanding of that which modern Westerners have commonly referred to as nature, or have otherwise thought of as the material world. Note that I'm *not* thinking here explicitly of the word "trinitarian" in terms of historic Christian doctrine, but in terms of a threefold historical meaning.

As I reflect about the material world with biblical faith in mind, I believe that that world can be understood as having *three dimensions*, which I have elsewhere called fabricated, cultivated, and wild nature—dimensions that typically come to their most visible public American expressions in familiar terms that I have already invoked: the city, the farm, and the wilderness.

But here I must offer a word of caution. These terms are so familiar that what might be called their existential impact often goes unnoticed. So, recognize that impact we must, if we are to grasp how problematic they can be, functionally, in our society today.

To this end, I'm now going to present some impressionistic notes about the place where I happen to live, the Boston area, as a kind of descriptive baseline for the theological proposal that is to follow. City, farm, and wilderness—each has a way of claiming many Americans existentially, and with considerable force. And it's important to recognize that characteristic of American culture.

III.

The city. Think of Boston's great cultural institutions, among them its sometimes elegantly designed universities, especially those situated along the winding Charles River. Think also of the historic beauty of Boston Commons, dating from 1634, thought to be the oldest park of its kind in the US. Or call to mind Boston's thousand-acre Emerald Necklace, a chain of grasslands, shrubs, and trees, running throughout the city, designed more than a hundred years ago by the eminent Frederick Law Olmsted.

This, however, is the same city that's now defined, in some measure, by its notorious Big Dig—designed by a committee, some wag once said—a massive, submerged highway project that reportedly cost more than $14.8 billion (in today's dollars) to construct, and which to this day is traversed by many thousands of polluting cars and trucks and buses twenty-four hours a day. Drivers in traffic jams on that Big Dig highway today are obviously not able to observe—perhaps not even able to think about—farm animals or vistas of distant mountains. Their world is the asphalt jungle, as it has sometimes been called, notwithstanding that overall Boston features some green spaces.

Even more than the lives of commuters, pavement circumscribes the lives of many lower-income Bostonians; in their neighborhoods tree canopies tend to be scarce, and concrete and blacktop are omnipresent: people who live in these places typically do not have the financial wherewithal to spend much time in the countryside or to undertake hiking or camping adventures in the mountains. The city, typically, is their island home, for better, for worse. For them, more often than not, the farm and the wilderness are little known experientially and therefore remain, for many, alien worlds.

In Boston, presiding over it all, is the city's famous—for some, infamous—cement city hall with its brutalistic architecture, along with that building's vast concrete plaza. If that urban installation doesn't tell the whole story of Boston's culture, it still has enormous symbolic power. Not surprisingly, then, for many who identify with the City of Boston, fabricated nature dominates their daily experience, whether they are residents or commuters.

IV.

The farm. Think of historic Brook Farm (on land currently within the Boston city limits), a short-lived Transcendentalist rural communitarian experiment in the 1840s, which idealistically accented intellectual discourse and hands-on agricultural labor for a few well-educated white New Englanders and also a number of craftspeople. Ralph Waldo Emerson was a founding member.

Nature for the Brook Farm community was a world of quiet beauty and, sometimes, hands-on care for plants and animals for the few who could afford to live in that kind of intentional setting. Members of that community consciously distanced themselves from what they thought of, even then, as the noise, the grime, and the turmoil of the city and from what was, for many of them, the dangerous or even hostile world of the wilderness far beyond.

Today's US farms typically differ markedly from Brook Farm, to be sure; they range from self-sustaining, organic projects in New England to vast Midwestern agribusiness enterprises. An example of the former is Noonday Farm in Wincheden, Massachusetts, inspired by the vision of Peter Mauren and the Catholic Worker movement and founded by Haley House, a Catholic food ministry in Boston. Clearly, farming in the US takes many forms.

But, notwithstanding such differences, the idea of farming still has its own compelling aura of meanings for many Americans, far beyond the hands-on work of farming itself. One might even argue that after World War II the development of suburbia in the US reflected a widespread green longing for the then disappearing—and thereafter idealized—"life on the farm." Along with all this, agrarianism has become a kind of metaphysical lens for some of its champions, through which to view the whole world, as in some, if not all, of the writings of Wendell Berry.

V.

The wilderness. Then of course there's Walden Pond, a few miles outside Boston, celebrated by the one who is now widely regarded as America's greatest champion of nature, the aforementioned Henry David Thoreau, especially in his masterpiece, *Walden*. While Thoreau took some engaged civic stands on occasion, his writings generally depict the city as an artificial, even destructive milieu for human life. He once said that there's more wisdom in (tiny, rural) Boxboro than in the whole of Boston. Thoreau was very much at home in his small-town, agricultural milieu in Concord, even when he was living at Walden Pond (he walked home each week to have his mother do his laundry).

Contrary to some popular images, too, for many years Thoreau was not a full-throated champion of the American wilderness. That attitude began to develop in a thoroughgoing way only after he returned from his harrowing climb to the top of Mount Katahdn, in Maine. But, rightly so, he remains America's most popular champion of what he thought of as wildness.

And vast numbers of Americans to this day aspire to follow in Thoreau's footsteps, even if they do not actually seek to live some kind of simple rustic life in the wilds, as Thoreau once imagined himself to be doing at Walden Pond. This aspiration achieves perhaps its most popular expression in the throngs that annually visit the nation's many national parks and in the highly esteemed wilderness backpacking expeditions undertaken by those of a certain age and social class, who often identify deeply with what they perceive to be the mystique of the mountains.

The same aspiration is also evident everywhere, for those who have eyes to see, in the historic romanticizing of Indigenous peoples and their life in what westernized peoples have come to think of as wilderness. This is symbolized perhaps most familiarly by omnipresent popular images of "the Indians" who emerged from the primeval forest to welcome newly arrived European settlers, as in the ubiquitously reproduced painting by Edward Hicks, *The Peaceable Kingdom*.

VI.

Interestingly, and perhaps soberingly, in our era each of these dimensions of the material world has been lifted up individually, at one time or another, by American theologians of some standing: the city by Harvey Cox; the farm by Norman Wirzba; the wilderness by Matthew Fox. Numerous lesser known figures have adopted similar theological programs. All this single-minded popular theologizing appears to me to be as American as apple pie. Such reflections mirror, in some significant measure, long-standing trends in popular American culture more generally.

In a sense, therefore, many Americans of European descent are living in a schizoid-like society today, various theologians included. Some claim the city as their center of value, some the farm, others the wilderness. And sometimes they do that single-mindedly, even with marked disparagement of the other two.

Which has led me to wonder over the years: given the existential weight of each of these centers of public value, *can most Americans really do otherwise than identify with only one of them?* And, if so, will not that continuingly pose justice issues for our society more generally? Which dimension is to be most highly valued? And which dimensions are to be of lesser value, even devalued? Is Nature's Nation, as understood by its citizens of European descent, therefore perpetually destined to be the land of trichotomous culture wars?

Not necessarily. It is not that difficult to embrace all three at the same time, I have discovered. With apologies to America and to apple pie, I have for some time proposed an integrative *theological* vision, which accents city, farm, and wilderness equally, from the redwood forest to the Gulf Stream waters.

And, with observations such as the following, I have maintained that that's the way the Scriptures as a whole appear to envision these things. The created world, for the Scriptures, has *three coequal dimensions,* which here I want to call, as I have already noted—trinitarian. And the God of biblical faith appears to want it to be precisely that way.

VII.

The city, again. Consider the central biblical theme that highlights the theological meanings of Jerusalem and the New Jerusalem. A theological tale of these two cities lies at the heart of many narratives in the Bible. Isaiah 40–55 includes a vision of all the peoples of the earth making a pilgrimage to a gloriously renewed Jerusalem, amid a pervasively transformed world of nature. The book of Revelation envisions a heavenly Jerusalem in the midst of a totally renovated creation.

The farm, again. Consider the biblical vision that in Genesis 2 shows primal humanity created to live in and to care for—not rule over—the Garden of Eden. Adam and Eve were created to be good farmers! Adam himself was specifically identified as being of the earth (*adamah*). For Genesis 2, caring for the earth and being of the earth is the normative human vocation. (In contrast, the first biblical creation narrative in Genesis 1 may best be read as belonging to the urbancentric view of creation I have previously described.)

When, more particularly, God brings the animals to Adam to name them, that naming should be regarded as an act of bonding, as when God gives Israel its name, not as some kind of domination. Not for nothing, also, does Noah take *all* the animals, the clean and the unclean, with him onto the ark. In this sense, Noah is exercising the primordial human—agricultural—vocation, according to this trajectory of biblical thought: to care for all the creatures of the earth.

The wilderness, again. Consider Job being thrust toward the wilds to contemplate the great wonders of God there (Job 38–41), and note that that experience was intended by God not as a punishment but as a gift of awe and a promise of new life. And consider the Gospel of Mark's account of Jesus being led by the Spirit into the wilderness to be with wild animals at the very beginning of his ministry (1:12–13)—not primarily to be tested, but to be revealed as the second Adam, the Divine-human Redeemer of the whole creation, who like the first Adam is at home in the Garden with the wild beasts.

Note, too, how this inclusive theme of human embeddedness in the whole creation—not just in the city, not just on the farm, surely not just in the wilderness—was given voice in a quite different manner by the apostle Paul in his Letter to the Colossians, 1:15ff., a text to which I will return at the very end of this book.

There we see that not just human history, but the existence of *all things*—some facets of which, for Paul, were thoroughly alien to human life—are held together and redeemed by the cosmic Christ, who is at once the head of the new redeemed human community and of the church in particular. We can say, then, that in Colossians Paul embraces theologically what for him was radically other—wild?—in the created world: the "principalities and powers" within the cosmology of his time.

So for me it makes perfect—biblical—sense *to celebrate city, farm, and wilderness together as coequal dimensions of God's good creation.* And it makes more particular—biblical—sense to contemplate city, farm, and wilderness together as differing expressions of God's creative and redemptive intentionality for the whole creation; and we can safely—biblically—hold the following assumptions: that each dimension of the material world has its own integrity before God, that any one dimension should never be viewed as ultimately more important than the other two, and that each will flourish eternally with the dawning of the eschatological new creation of all things.

VIII.

Note the theological assumptions I'm working with here. The city and the farm and the wilderness all have their own value, *equal* value in biblical perspective. But note, all the more so, that this value is *derivative*. God is *the* center of value. Each dimension of the created world depends for its ultimate standing on *the* Value-Giver, who sees that the created world is good, both as a whole and in its rich dimensionality, both now and in the world to come.

But note well, also: each of these dimensions, as the Scriptures also make abundantly clear, is in fact riven with ambiguities. A complete analysis of the three, for sure, would explore those ambiguities. Thus we daily encounter egregious examples of human-on-human violence in cities and farm communities, sometimes even in wilderness settings. Then there are the vast patterns of human destructiveness, in our time typically driven by corporate interests that negatively impact life-sustaining ecosystems on our planet—leaving us today with our horrendous, global climate crisis, among other planetary disorders.

Beyond that, recall the violence that sometimes dramatically unfolds in the wilds or in larger planetary settings. Sometimes this is called "natural evil." It is particularly evident in the bloody dynamics of the food chain on our planet, but it is all the more dramatically apparent in phenomena like volcanic eruptions or tsunamis. Coming to terms theologically with such ambiguities in each of nature's dimensions is obviously critically important, but I have cautiously bypassed detailed discussions of such matters here

IX.

Here I have only wanted to address a much more modest theological challenge, which I believe is nevertheless well worth pondering. I have wanted to find a way to say to Nature's Nation, particularly to Euro-American urbanists and agrarians and wilderness advocates, and also to all those American Christians of any background who have been thoroughly enculturated in this respect: never mind being a champion of the city *or* the farm *or* the wilderness. *How about three cheers for all three*? How about three cheers for the trinitarian richness of nature that we experience on planet Earth, even if that might make us feel—rightly or even just slightly—"un-American?"

VI

What's the Best Way to Shrink Your Carbon Footprint?

NOT TOO LONG AGO, the *New York Times* provided a pop quiz to invite answers to this now familiar question. It cited a dozen oft-discussed eco-acts aimed to help with that shrinking, such as turning down the heat at night during the winter. Which *is* the best?[1]

I.

Okay, *mea culpa*, first of all. I've been writing about ecological—and related theological and justice—issues since the middle of the last century. *I* ought to know the correct answers to such carbon footprint questions, right? And sure, I did get nine of twelve right. But I *under*estimated, by one step each, the value of what the *Times* article considered to be *the three most important planetary practices* for shrinking your carbon footprint: living car-free, using renewable electricity, and eating a vegan diet.

No wonder, I suppose, because I'm not in a position, if the truth be known, to make any serious progress on any of those

---

1. Sander van der Linden, "Quiz: What's the Best Way to Shrink Your Carbon Footprint?" Opinion, *New York Times*, December 15, 2022, https://www.nytimes.com/interactive/2022/12/15/opinion/how-reduce-carbon-footprint-climate-change.html/.

three major lifestyle fronts, much as I would like to. Living car-free, for example. Anywhere other than New York City or comparable urban settings: good luck on that one. Except for such exceptions, the car-free life won't work for most Americans today, even—or especially—for the working poor, who sometimes have to drive many miles in secondhand cars to get to their places of employment. Me? I very much "need" my car, given the way that the affluent world in which I have chosen to live is organized. *Mea culpa*, again.

So taking that pop quiz seems to have left me in a familiar fix: pondering my ecoguilt. I addressed that topic at one point in my book *EcoActivist Testament*. There I resolved to forget about ecoguilt altogether and just try to get on with something ecologically responsible. Following up on that discussion, these further thoughts cross my mind.

Forget about shrinking your carbon footprint for a while and *find some leverage*. Remember what you learned in high school physics about how a lever works? Here are three current examples: two from politics and one from religion. All along, let's hear it for the leverage!

II.

Politics. The enormously impressive, card-carrying Methodist activist Bill McKibben, whom I mention often in this book, has launched a new nationwide movement for folks like me, Third Act. The rationale behind it is that many in older generations in the US have now left behind the demanding stages of finding a life's path and then beginning to walk that path.

Many of us in our greying years have by now settled down for the long haul—or even have retired. (I've been retired for more than twenty years.) We've found some financial stability along the way, too, many of us; some have even made a lot of money. So, argues McKibben, now's the time for us in these older generations to pitch in eagerly with financial assets and boots on the ground to address our global climate crisis, especially since we all care so much about the world that our grandchildren are going to inherit.

Why not then throw ourselves into collective efforts like McKibben's Third Act right now, as much as we possibly can? This kind of thing is called, as I have observed, *leverage*. A political movement can sometimes have an outsized impact.

So, yes, I will keep trying to find ways regularly to eat less meat, say, or to drive the miles that I have concluded that I must drive as efficiently as I possibly can. In this sense, I believe that we all are called by God to do everything at once, in these times of crisis. But, if I may say so, God prefers politics—rightly done, of course. Hence I'm highlighting Third Act here.

Here is another political example. It's better to work with a public splash of fellow alums or fellow students to get your college to divest of Exxon stock, say, than to focus on convincing your spouse or your roommate to join with you to eat lower on the food chain or to give up meat altogether. I've already mentioned my own—surely modest—efforts to participate in group actions against my own college, actions that were, thankfully, organized not by me but by people who knew what they were doing. It's best, of course, do everything; but first throw yourself into the world of politics, like that divestment struggle, if you possibly can. Go for the leverage.

III.

Religion. If you belong to a community of faith, as I do, I recommend that you check out how you can leverage things in this context, too, if you haven't already figured that out. See if you can have a multiplier effect for ecojustice by more consistently participating in your own religious community regionally or even nationally, where cadres of faithful souls are probably already at work, protesting or lobbying or building coalitions. Get some political leverage for ecojustice by working with other people of faith.

I have tried to do this in my own denominational setting, by supporting as much as I can an outstanding grassroots, faith-driven ecojustice movement that I have already mentioned in this book a number of times: Lutherans Restoring Creation (LRC). In *EcoActivist Testament,* as I have also already noted, I list a number of such religious groups.[2] By working with and through one of these groups, you can have a leveraging effect politically that might astound you, especially when all those groups work together, as they regularly do.

I have even fantasized that the whole ecumenical community in the US, sparked by its own faith-driven ecojustice activists, could join together to confront McDonald's! What if an ecumenical coalition of church groups were publicly to announce that they were asking all their members to stop eating Big Macs and also that they were demanding that McDonald's reinstate its vegetarian McPlants? Why? This is much more than a lifestyle issue.

Frankly, American meat-eating habits are a major part of a trend that's undercutting a number of our planet's ecosystems. "If Americans continue to average three burgers a week while the developing world starts to follow our path," one report has convincingly argued, "it's hard to see how the Amazon survives."[3]

The Amazon? Yes, because corporate interests are greedily cutting down larger and larger portions of Amazon forests in order to provide more grazing land for beef cattle, which the US market is constantly and urgently demanding. At the same time, the whole Amazon region is "the lungs of our planet," as it often has been described. Those forests spectacularly sequester huge amounts of CO_2 and purify the air as they do. Hence this lamentable ecologic: the more Big Macs, the more Amazon trees cut down, the more CO_2 in the air, and the more destructive the global warming of our earthly home.

This dream, then. You're going to figure out how to join a nationwide faith coalition—yet to be launched—to end the Big Mac

2. H. Paul Santmire, *EcoActivist Testament* (Eugene, OR: Cascade Books, 2022), 1–2.

3 Michael Grunwald, "No One Wants to Say 'Put Down That Burger,' but We Really Should," Guest Essay, Opinion, *New York Times,* December 15, 2022, https://www.nytimes.com/2022/12/15/opinion/food-diets-meat-biodiverstiy-cop15.html/.

in favor of reinstating the discontinued McPlant. You're going to resolve, more generally, to protest against McDonald's itself, pressuring that company to end its orders for Amazonian beef and to beef up its marketing of reinstated McPlants. Picket McDonald's anyone?

Imagine this. You're going to lobby your own congregation's leadership to allow you, or some other congregational member or group of members, to take your confirmation class to the nearest Mickey Dees to get into the action. Such a project might well spark some good ecojustice discussions, even some helpful controversy, back in your own congregation the following Sunday and—hopefully—some notice in the local media. And more.

What if *all* the confirmation classes in your district or your diocese or your synod were to join in? Fill a score of McDonald's parking lots for a couple of hours one Saturday with young church protesters who have studied the issue! Maybe ask those kids themselves to write the press releases and to be prepared for the press interviews! For the sake of their religious education! Hear and see this, then, on the local nightly news—all those confirmands chanting, again and again: "No Big Macs—Yes McPlants! Save the Am-a-zon!"

Later, this kind of public protest could be duplicated all over the country, led by green people of faith of all ages who have long been eagerly searching for some tangible way to get into the action. Count me in.

IV.

Conclusion. Isn't the kind of leveraging ecoactivist participation in politics and in religion that I have just described *the best way*, if not the only way, to shrink your carbon footprint? Methinks, yes.

VII

How to Be a Christian Citizen in These Times of Crisis

THIS IS A HUGE theme, of course. My angle? Turn to the Bible (!). So I now want to reclaim and reapply some conventional-sounding words from the apostle Paul's Letter to the Galatians, words which have long given a boost to my own faith. I hope that these words, by one of Christianity's foremost interpreters, will give you a boost, too, as you also keep trying to figure out how to be a Christian citizen in these times of crisis.

I.

Paul's been dealing with a bunch of controversies that were tearing the Galatian church apart. You can almost hear him sigh, as he tries to pull it altogether at the very end of his letter. "And," Paul says, with a tonality that might sound like your grandmother's voice when you went away to college for the first time, *"let us not be weary in well-doing"* (Galatians 6:9 KJV).

But forget about your grandmother's good counsel. Paul has a much more commanding thought. This is the whole text: *"So let us not be weary in well doing; for we will reap at harvest time, if we don't give up. So then, whenever we have an opportunity, let us work for the good of all, and especially for those of the family of faith."* (Galatians 6:9–10 my translation).

II.

Here is a vignette. For my own vocational reasons, in recent years I've embarked on a personal mission: to interview, thanks to Zoom, some Christians who are at the frontlines of the church's mission today, dealing with global ecojustice issues. One of the people I spoke with was a young pastor in Nigeria. At the time, he was enrolled via Zoom in a certificate program in global environmental issues at my church's theological seminary in California.

Only three years into his ministry, he was then dealing with a world of enormous disruption. The forests all around his parish had been devastated by logging and then by severe erosion. Food sources had become unreliable. And the struggle, sometimes violent, between Christians and Muslims had been unrelenting.

In *that* situation, the apostle Paul's injunction not to be weary in well doing might be taken to be as clear as the day is long. I mean, support one another, heal the land, make peace with your neighbors. Momentous things like that. The situation there is so bad and so clear, or so it seemed to me from a distance, that you can just get on with the Christian life, day by day, without much thought about it.

But what could Paul's words mean for American churchgoers in the rather conventional, even comfortable, situation that we occupy today in the good old USA? Imagine a typical Fourth of July. To think of my own region, half of New England wants to go to the beach on the Fourth. That's often what's on *our* minds.

How can *we* be Christian citizens, then, when the challenges that we face don't seem to be nearly so immediate or so pressing as those in places like Nigeria?

III.

Let me get at it this way. And here I have an observation that you might have learned at some point in a Bible class, an observation that first-year theology students typically cherish. In New Testament Greek, there are two words for "time," *chronos* and *kairos*.

The first is clock time: *chronos*, as in "chronology." What year did Columbus "discover" America? Or as comedian Dick Gregory liked to say: in what year did those people on the shore start waving at Columbus's three ships? That's chronos time—1492.

Kairos time is something else. *Kairos* time is when you go out to harvest your lettuce before it bolts. *Kairos* time is when your baby's about to be born. *Kairos* time is when you pass the word that there's going to be a meeting to figure out how to deal with the likes of Columbus and his kind.

In his Letter to the Galatians, Paul uses the word *kairos* as a matter of course. First, implicitly, by his reference to—harvest time: *"So let us not grow weary in well doing, for we will reap at harvest time . . ."* That's verse 9 of Galatians, chapter 6. The harvest happens on *kairos* time.

Then there's verse 10: *"So then,"* says the flat English translation we regularly have before us, *"whenever we have an opportunity, let us work for the good of all, and especially for those of the family of faith."* The Greek here is actually *kairos*, meaning: *"whenever the time's right, let's go for it, for the good of all . . ."*—and so on.

IV.

Some questions now.

What *kairos* is God giving *you* at this point in your life? What *kairos* is God giving *us* American Christians—as community of faith—right now? Maybe something about helping with your congregation's homeless shelter? Maybe something related to politics and the Supreme Court? Or, say, finding yet another way to protest climate change? Perhaps some international church initiative that's geared to address global poverty, viewed against the background of climate change? Not to speak of how you're going to vote in the next presidential election.

Those are the kinds of questions, I propose, that you and I will want to keep asking as we keep thinking about not being weary in well-doing. Where's the *kairos* moment? Is this the right time? And if it is, are we up to it?

V.

Many years ago, I was given the opportunity—I was given the *kairos*—to be part of a biracial American church delegation of men and women whose assignment was to visit Black Lutheran congregations in South Africa and Namibia. It was at the height of the apartheid crisis. It was a harrowing experience for all of us Americans, especially when we visited the huge Black township, Soweto. Armored trucks of white soldiers were cruising around everywhere. We were told never to take a photo.

I had one afternoon off in Soweto, and I decided to hail a cab and go out to the headquarters of the South African Council of Churches, to check the place out and maybe to meet people. To my surprise, when I arrived, a large and chaotic meeting was just about to begin. People, almost all of them Black South Africans, were milling around all over the place. There was a stirring in the air. I sat in the back, in one of the few seats that were still available. Up front was a panel of ecumenical Black clergy, led by a Lutheran pastor, Simon Farasani.

Turns out, I had stumbled into a controversial meeting of global significance, when the South African Council of Churches was releasing what it called its *Kairos Document*. Among other things, that document said: the time has come for all Christians in South Africa to openly resist the tyranny of the minority white government. It was a *kairos* moment that I'll never forget.

Has the time arrived—has the *kairos* arrived—for you and for me to sign on to a new *Kairos Document*? Has the *kairos* come for you and for me to stand up to resist neofascist trends in our own society? To get out into the streets perchance? As eminent conservative jurist

Michael Luttig reportedly told the January 6th committee a while ago, as he thought about the then current threats to our democracy: "I would have laid my body across the road before I would have let the vice president overturn the 2020 election."[1] Some think that the *kairos* has come for us to do just that. Others think that we may be close to such a *kairos*. What do *you* think?

While you're thinking about that—that kind of dramatic *kairos* moment—keep in mind that the *kairos* that the Spirit's offering you at this time of your life might also be mundane, as the world counts such things.

Some years ago, I joined members of my own congregation in a slow march down Mass Ave from Cambridge to the Boston Common in order to demand climate justice, joining many others from a whole range of backgrounds. No big deal, in a certain sense. But for me it was a *kairos* moment.

You can fill in the blanks in your own life. Lord knows, maybe when you took what you thought at the time was that modest step for justice, you were in fact and in faith responding to a *kairos* moment that God was giving you. Even writing a letter or signing a petition or cutting a check! Keep up the good work. Keep searching for such *kairos* moments.

VI.

Finally now: how can you do it? How can I do it? How could that Nigerian pastor do it or Pastor Simon Farasani? How can anyone find the spiritual wherewithal to be a Christian citizen in such wrenching times? Maybe dangerous times, even for us.

This is my answer. You don't have to go it alone. I don't have to go it alone. All we need to do is to let ourselves get carried away in the Spirit, by the good news of Jesus, again and again, in the midst of the congregation where we worship.

---

1. Hon. J. Michael Luttig, testimony in Hearing before the Select Committee to Investigate the January 6th Attack on the US Capitol, 117th Cong., 2nd session, June 16, 2022, page 15. https://www.congress.gov/117/chrg/CHRG-117hhrg49351/CHRG-117hhrg49351.pdf/.

Consider another biblical text here, from Mark's Gospel, about this Liberator—capital *L*—this Divine-Human Liberator, sent from God at just the right time, *the Kairos* of every other *kairos*. This is my translation of Mark's words: "Jesus came to Galilee . . . saying, 'The *Kairos* is fulfilled, and the Reign of God has come near; turn around and believe in the good news" (Mark 1:15).

In a word: God gives you this Kairos. God gives me this Kairos. This cosmic Liberator, Jesus, called the Christ! All you and I have to do is to give up business-as-usual and claim this Kairos as our own. And then we'll find ourselves empowered by the Spirit to respond to every other *kairos* moment that God gives us along the way. That's the biblical promise, I believe. *The* Kairos is fulfilled and *the* Reign of God has come near; turn around from your depression or your fear and believe! Get with the good news of Jesus!

VII.

So you do the right thing every time you decide to worship on Sundays. You turn away from your ordinary experience. You take your stand with the Jesus people for that Sunday *kairos*, either in person or by Zooming in. This is the first step of Christian citizenship, I believe: you get with *the* Kairos, this fulfilled time, the mission of Jesus, as you identify with the followers of Jesus.

Then, in the Spirit of Jesus, you'll be ready to respond to any other *kairos* that God may be giving you along the way, horrendous or mundane or somewhere in between. Any day might be your harvest time, or mine. Just don't give up. Keep looking for that *kairos*. And keep welcoming the support that your own household of faith can offer you as you look and as you respond.

This, I believe, is what the Apostle is exhorting us to do. Ponder it now in a translation that I've revised for your sake and mine: "*So let's not be weary in well doing, for we will reap at harvest time, if we don't give up. So then, whenever God gives us a* kairos, *let us work for the good of all, and especially for those of the family of faith.*" That, I believe, is how to be a Christian citizen in *our* times of crisis.

PART THREE

Spiritual Explorations

VIII

The Avocado and the Onion
Two Spiritualities

MY WIFE AND I recently celebrated our fifty-sixth anniversary. Our children and grandchildren, thankfully, made it possible for us to do it. That event later gave me occasion to revisit a conversation that she and I have had over the years about our own spiritualities.

I've thought a lot about conjugal spirituality and even written about it. But I haven't yet told the whole truth, at least in public. This is what I propose to do here, with the following idiosyncratic spiritual reflections, as an encouragement for you to revisit the dynamics of your own spirituality and to see what you can see, afresh, whether you're married or single.

Somewhere in the midst of our long, beautiful, and, on occasion, stressful married life, my wife and I started to compare notes about our own spiritual lives. I don't recall which one of us came up with the image, but this, for better, for worse, for richer, for poorer, is it. Spiritually, she's more like an avocado and I'm more like an onion. Got that?

Part Three: Spiritual Explorations

I.

She has a solid spiritual center, pretty much summed up by the words often attributed to John Wesley which she learned in Sunday school: "Do all the good you can, in all the ways you can, to all the souls you can, in every place you can, at all the times you can, with all the zeal you can, as long as ever you can." Constantly and fervently seeking to embrace the good—that's the heart of the matter, for her.

I perceive myself as having a number of inner spiritual layers, onion-like, but with *nothing* at the core of my being. Do I think that my innermost self is nothingness? I suppose that I do. That thought may sound strange, but I'm inspired by it, as I often recall the traditional Christian teaching that God creates the world out of nothing (*ex nihilo*). Nothingness, in that sense, for me, is the place were God dwells. So I welcome the confluence of inwardness and nothingness.

While I certainly affirm Wesley's words about doing good, then, I experience my inmost self as fragmented and unstable and centerless, rather than as integrated and solid to the core. I'm very much attuned to Martin Luther's words on his deathbed: "We are all beggars."

I also resonate with Luther in a different key too: when asked what he would do if the world were coming to an end, he reportedly replied, memorably, with these oft-quoted words, which I have already stated in this book: "I would plant an apple tree." Miserable sinner that I am, I love to plant trees, in spite of it all.

II.

More, then, on our marriage. Early on, Laurel found herself swept up by presidential campaign of George McGovern. She was driven inwardly to embrace that political good—McGovern's dedication to social justice. So she went door-to-door in Precinct G in Wellesley, Massachusetts, and single-handedly—so it seemed to me at the time—delivered that precinct for the candidate who was then to lose so resoundingly across the country. While I cheered for her every step of the way as she did her thing, at that time I found myself in a different place.

In those days, I was intensely engaged at my desk in research about the theology of nature and about how a whole class of relatively well-off Americans had come so to idolize nature, especially the wilderness, that they had forgotten about the needs of the poor in US cities. Be that as it may, at that time my wife was the solid activist and I was more or less the solitary page-turner, sometimes lost in my thoughts.

On the other hand, I don't want to push the avocado and onion analogy too far. Laurel and I have had many days, beginning already early in our marriage, when each one of us has felt like the other, in this respect. Thus, from the start, she has been an engaged but introspective reader of countless novels while, early on, I was becoming something of a '60s activist, a habit that I have tried to cultivate ever since. For us, it never has been just avocado or onion, doing good or losing oneself in thought. But I think that the analogy is revealing and, I hope, instructive as a way of thinking about what the spiritual life can be for followers of Jesus.

III.

That's *the* point, actually, that I have come to realize over the years. Sometimes it *has* taken me a while to discover the obvious: that the challenge of *following Jesus* is what the spiritual life for people like Laurel and me is most fundamentally about, not so much about our interiority, but first and foremost about our discipleship.

And more. Instructed by Laurel's activism and becoming increasingly aware of my own introspective habits over the years, I have come to believe that following Jesus has two dimensions: what we are called *to do* and what we are called *to see*. I want to illustrate this point by highlighting the theological discipleship of two of my faith heroes, Dietrich Bonhoeffer and Joseph Sittler.

Bonhoeffer is currently the better known of the two. As readers of this book, will probably already have noticed, I myself

Part Three: Spiritual Explorations

frequently allude to Bonhoeffer's widely read—if not always well followed—book *The Cost of Discipleship*. There Bonhoeffer lifts up the Sermon on the Mount as the bedrock of Christian identity. And, of course, Bonhoeffer's life story, especially his death while participating in the plot to assassinate Hitler, is rightly and widely celebrated.

For Sittler, I think, a good place to begin is the volume *Evocations of Grace: The Writings of Joseph Sittler on Ecology, Theology, and Ethics* (edited by Steven Bouma-Prediger and Peter Bakken).[1] Sittler is perhaps best known for his celebrations of Jesus as "the cosmic Christ," as the One in whom all things in our universe are held together: the vast world of universal nature as well as the particularities of human history here on planet Earth, and especially the very particular witness of the church; see Colossians 1:15ff., a key text for Sittler, and one that I will return to at the end of this book.

Early in his life, for example, spurred on by that kind of cosmic vision, Sittler wrote a passionate essay of lament for Lake Michigan, which at that time was being polluted beyond belief. There he also celebrated his love for Lake Michigan, almost in spousal terms.[2]

With Bonhoeffer and Sittler in mind, then, let me take you to church, with this question. Who is this Christ whom we worship every Sunday? Answer: the One announced in the Sermon on the Mount and the One proclaimed by the cosmic witness of the Letter to the Colossians: the One whom the Holy Scriptures bid us to take up our crosses to follow and the One whom the same Scriptures also invite us to celebrate in thought, word, and deed as the Savior of "all things," the Mediator of cosmic salvation. This duplex Jesus, if I may put it that way, is the divine-human Servant who

---

1. Joseph Sittler, *Evocations of Grace: The Writings of Joseph Sittler on Ecology, Theology, and Ethics*, ed. Steve Bouma-Prediger and Peter Bakken (Grand Rapids: Eerdmans, 2000).

2. Joseph Sittler, *Running with the Hounds: Conversations with Campus Ministry*, edited by Galen Hors (Chicago: Department of Campus Ministry of the Evangelical Lutheran Church in America, 1977), 95.

creates and sustains our duplex spiritualities, active and reflective, solid-cored and lightly layered.

IV.

This, then, is my invitation to anyone who will listen. *Do or see—so that you can do and see.* Inspired by teachers like Bonhoeffer and Sittler, aspire spiritually to be an earthbound disciple or a cosmic dreamer, and then discover that instructed by the Scriptures, you can blessedly be both, to one degree or another.

To that end, you might even want to think of yourself primarily according to the image of an avocado or primarily according to the image of an onion, at any given time. This analogy doesn't sound very profound, I know, but it has worked for Laurel and for me for a long time, and I recommend it.

IX

Cutting through the Ice to Encounter the Depths

LATE IN THE FALL, Laurel and I typically shut down our Maine farmhouse in the eastern foothills of the White Mountains. We're not skiers, but even if we were and we wanted to do some skiing at some nearby resorts, it would be folly for us to stay in that old house, which dates from the mid-1800s, during the winter.

The issue: during the bitter winter months, keeping the water in the pipes of that porous structure from freezing. We once rented out the place for the skiing season, and the pipes kept freezing all the time, even with the furnace constantly on and the woodstove blazing as much as possible. So we have to drain all the water from the pipes in our house, before we close it down for the winter months.

Still, one or two times during the winter we do travel up to that frigid place for a couple of days. Sometimes I wonder why.

I.

It's all the more puzzling when I reflect on what we have to do in order to travel there in midwinter and on what we have to do while we're there, simply to maintain ourselves. Our Prius barely handles the up-and-down, twisting rural roads, covered as they often are with snow and ice. One time in the middle of winter, in order to

Cutting through the Ice to Encounter the Depths

head home, we had to start out by driving downhill for two miles, which was the wrong direction for us, in order to take a tediously circuitous route to get us back on track heading south, our direction of choice.

But I'll begin at the beginning. Even though I wonder why we visit our place in the ice and snow, let me tell you what happens when we first pull up to that Maine house in the dark of winter, which is the time we usually arrive. Before anything else can happen, using the small, sturdy US Army shovel that I've brought along, I have to chop my way some twenty feet from the street to the front door, typically through deep, iced-over drifts.

Then we lug in not only our modest provisions but also a half dozen gallons of water for drinking and cooking. As soon as possible, we begin to burn precious stacks of firewood lavishly in our Franklin stove, around which we then huddle. This, in order to keep ourselves warm, of course, but also to keep those jugs of water from freezing. First thing the next morning, it's time for me to cut a hole in the ice on the little stream out back. Why?

We have to use the toilet while we're there, of course, but there's no way to flush it during the winter, since the water pipes in the house have been drained. On the other hand, we need the water that we carried in from home for drinking and cooking. To deal with the toilet-flushing challenge, then, I put on my boots, grab hold of a long-handled, sharp-edged spade, a small pitcher, and a couple of buckets. I then crunch my way through the deep snow behind our house for a hundred feet or so to a tiny stream that's totally covered by high drifts. Precariously, I inch my way down the almost indiscernible snow-covered bank of that stream to the underlying ice, which is maybe two or three inches thick.

Once balanced over the ice, I use my spade as an ice pick to chop a foot-square opening. I then hunker down over that opening, and contemplate the water that flows there, maybe eight inches deep, flowing along even when the temperature has dropped to below zero. It must be a comic apparition, were anyone to witness it. There I hover, pitcher in hand, wind raging around me, bailing out water from beneath the ice, in order to fill the two buckets that I've brought with me.

Witness me, then, cautiously carrying a single bucket of nearly frozen water, crunching through the snowpack to the back door of our house. Then I repeat the process. Once, by the time I arrived at the house with the second bucket, a skin of new ice had already formed on the first bucket. Even when the sun might be beaming down, the ferocious winter temperatures rule the day, and permeate my hands through my double-gloves. All this, so that we can flush the toilet with that stream water when we need to.

II.

But why? Why not remain at home in our well-heated condominium in the Boston area and warmly continue to embrace our comfortable, retired existence? Why push ourselves, in this way, to confront the elements? Yes, there's something to be said about being inside, near the roaring Franklin stove, in the evening. It's a "comfy" experience, as a friend once suggested, a time when "the weather outside is frightful, but the fire is so delightful." There is indeed something to be said about what one historian of American culture once called, perhaps sardonically, "the American quest for contentment in 'the bourgeois interior.'" But be that as it may, why rural Maine in the winter?

One of the factors, on my part, could be my years. Well past eighty now, am I secretly regarding myself as some kind of heroic, wilderness warrior? Is this an old-age rite or even some kind of masculine thing, to show myself that "I can still do it"? But I think that it's more than that kind of stereotypical posturing.

III.

Could the real lure of this adventure, for me, be that experience of chopping through the ice and seeing the *moving water* underneath? What *do* I see? Even though the stream is only eight inches deep, I'm overcome by an experience that Paul Tillich often called "the dimension of depth." I took courses with Tillich for six years when I was an undergraduate and then beyond, and the experience of his voice haunts me to this day.

My God! In chilling midwinter, underneath all those drifts and that thick ice, *reality is moving*. It's flowing. It's going somewhere. We don't live entombed in a world destined for nothing but ice, at the cosmic end of all things. Underneath it all, Being *is* Becoming, not Stasis—and death.

Granted, this particular encounter with the Depths of Being and Becoming is only twelve inches square and eight inches deep. But stay with me. It's a revelation for me when I chop through the ice, under those arctic conditions, to discover that flowing water. To some passerby, it might look odd. It feels odd. Still, I there and then regard myself, when I stand there, as contemplating the Depths.

IV.

I have only lately come to that probably comical, but to me heartfelt spiritual conclusion. Recently on a family outing to celebrate my daughter-in-law's graduation from a professional leadership-training program at Dartmouth College, I was able to find occasion to wander through that institution's art museum. There I encountered, for the first time, works by the contemporary Finnish American New England painter Eric Aho. (That I later secured his permission to affix copies of his paintings to the covers of three of my books is another story for another time.)

A number of Aho's striking abstract, impressionist works depict three-by-four-foot squares cut through eight-inch ice at the edge of a sizeable, snow-covered New England pond. The most obvious explanation: those squares in the ice depict an opening into which someone who has just come from the sauna can plunge. Is Aho of Finnish heritage? Are the Finns known for their saunas?

The curator of that exhibit just didn't get it. She interpreted those paintings in terms of lines, colors, shapes, and contrasts. "Aho intuitively understood the hole as an abstract motif," she wrote in the visitor's guide. "The depth of the ice, the light of the day, the reflectivity or opaqueness of the water, the snow accumulating around the opening, and the angle of the view on the ice cut—all of these elements differentiate the paintings in terms of subject."[1] Really?

I saw much more. Most of the icy water squares in that exhibit were dark, although one was a bright yellow, as if reflecting sunlight. I found this series of dramatic water-squares in the pond ice powerful, a testimony to ultimate meanings, to Darkness and to Light. In this respect, I think, I remain a student of Tillich.

Tillich would have celebrated those paintings much more insightfully than the curator of that exhibit did. For Tillich, there is a darkness, a mystery, even a danger, to our world: Being threatened by Non-Being, yet not without offering moments of mystical elation. Tillich believed—and often demonstrated—that art can reveal those dynamics, that good art, more generally, can be a matter of what he called "ultimate concern," not just a matter of images, colors, contrasts, and lines, however striking they might be configured in any given work.

V.

Especially these paintings, for me! The curator made nothing of the whole sauna experience, surely presupposed by the artist. I couldn't believe it! Consider that experience. This is how my friend David Gagne, to whom this book is dedicated, recalls some of his own sauna moments, in the awesomely frigid world of northern Minnesota in winter. This, from a personal communication, used with his permission:

> After running out of the hot sauna, your naked body steaming in the below-zero weather, only your feet

---

1. Katherine Hart, Introduction, in *Eric Aho Ice Cuts* (Hanover, NH: Hood Museum of Art, Dartmouth College, 2016), 4; published in conjunction with an exhibition of the same title, organized and presented by the Hood Museum of Art, January 9–March 13, 2016, https://hoodmuseum.dartmouth.edu/sites/hoodmuseum.prod/files/hoodmuseum/publications/eric-aho_ice-cuts-bro.pdf/.

covered by socks to keep your feet from sticking to the ice, you jump into the hole in the ice (don't think about it—just do it—thinking is a problem at that point), dip under the water surface two or three times and then climb up the wood ladder leaning against the far edge of the rectangular hole. You always do this in pairs so another set of hands is there to grab you and pull you out in case you panic or somehow end up under the ice. (Alas, because of my stents I no longer can do this. Now I tend the fire, sit in the sauna, but can only go out and stand on the small deck of the sauna and let my body steam away the heat until I am cool enough to head back into the sauna again.) You actually don't feel cold when you go into the water—just your body feeling pin-prickles and the sucking sound as you try to breathe as you dip under the surface of the water.

It doesn't take a historian of religion to come up with the idea that that plunging into the dark freezing waters through that square hole cut in the ice and then resurfacing is a kind of death and resurrection experience, at some level of the conscious or unconscious mind. Into the cold depths of death you go and then out you come—alive! And exhilarated!

VI.

Don't Aho's water-square paintings suggest death and resurrection? Even Baptism? If they're not intended to recall dying and rising with Christ, surely they do suggest some kind of primal death and rebirth from the womb of the Depths.

I have concluded—oh so strangely, perhaps—that that's the vision that claims me, as I chop through that thick ice on that little stream behind our Maine house. It's a matter of ultimate concern. That's the underlying reason, doubtless among others, I have decided, why I keep wanting us to undertake those winter excursions to rural Maine, so that I can chop through that ice to contemplate those flowing Depths, comically perhaps, but powerfully for me.

X

Natural Images for Contemplating the Trinity

MARTIN LUTHER ONCE REFLECTED, in his own down-to-earth way, about how to instruct new believers who already have faith in God as the Father, but who do not as yet believe in the whole Trinity. First, Luther said, encourage them to believe in a second person, the Son, as well as the Father. Then, having grasped the idea of more than one Divine person, said Luther, it will be much easier for them also to believe in yet another, the Spirit (!). That approach could work, I imagine, probably not for Unitarians, but perhaps for others.

I.

Be that as it may, I have learned over the years that invoking *images* to help us engage God as the Trinity can be much more fruitful for such conversations than reflecting about *numbers*, whether one, two, and three or three-in-one. True, not all images will work well. A case in point: the image of three interlocking circles, which was displayed prominently in the sanctuary of the congregation in which I grew up, during what was then called "The Trinity Season."

It so happened that in those days a major American brewery, Ballantine Beer, had chosen that very image for its own marketing,

Natural Images for Contemplating the Trinity

with the slogan: "Purity, Body, and Flavor." Still, beer or no beer, a three-circled, geometrical image, for reasons that I don't fully understand, has never really commended itself to me.

Then, of course, there are ordinary *human* images for the Trinity. Consider, for example, the large oil painting by an unknown medieval artist long on display in Boston's Museum of Fine Arts, a painting that I've contemplated, with mixed feelings, many times. That work depicts the traditional image of a great king, who is wearing a stately gold crown and colorful robes and displaying a long white beard.

That King—and it *is* a king, which the patriarchal Christianity of the Middle Ages took for granted—is depicted as sitting on a majestic throne and holding a large figure of the crucified Son before him, the Son with his head bowed in holy repose, his anguished body nailed to his cross. Up in the right-hand corner of that painting, all by itself, almost invisible, you can see a tiny figure of a white dove, which of course was intended to represent the Holy Spirit. For a whole range of good reasons, I believe, that medieval vision of the Trinity has always troubled me.

Should we, then, regard *any* attempt to present the Trinity *visually* to be a fool's errand? I don't think so. Before we find ourselves driven to abandon the quest to identify images for the Trinity altogether, I want to remind you that I, for one, have suggested, over the years, especially in my book *Ritualizing Nature: Renewing Christian Liturgy in a Time of Crisis* (2008), that by drawing on *images from nature* we can grasp some of the deeper meanings of our encounters with the Trinity in a fresh way, even as we may well want to keep highlighting images from human life, like father and son or love between persons more generally.

So in *Ritualizing Nature*, I propose an image of the Niagara River, its awe-inspiring Falls and its majestic downstream gorges that are full of tumultuous and terrifying currents, to help us more fully to grasp the mystery of the Trinity. I still recommend that particular natural image to anyone who has eyes of faith and who wants to see still more.

II.

Here I want to propose yet another natural image—or a set of images, actually—for the Trinity, which has lately dawned on me, for your consideration. See what you think about it. This is how it happened: I turned my desk chair around. There, affixed to the shelves of a bookcase, I saw prints of three extraordinary paintings.

I had put those prints in place, over the years, with no particular theological purpose consciously in mind. I had them in my collection and I wanted to display them. That was that. I displayed them simply because each one spoke to me. In retrospect, now, I have concluded that a certain trinitarian logic was unfolding in my mind's eye in that process, however subliminally.

One advantage of contemplating these reproductions together in this way, I now realize, is that they are so obviously what they are: varied representations of the beauty and the wildness and the grandeur and, on occasion, the glorious peace of the natural world itself. Hence it should be clear that these images are not *literally* depicting God, surely not as that aforementioned medieval painting had been designed to do. Yet with the eyes of faith, I believe, taken together these images can be read, figuratively, as revealing testimonies to the Trinity.

III.

Contemplate first, then, the image in a large oil painting, *Weatherbeaten* (1894), by Winslow Homer, which I happen to have seen on numerous occasions at the Portland, Maine, Museum of Art. I read this painting as—whatever other meanings it might be speaking—inspired, although not intended, testimony to the mystery of the first person of the Trinity. God the Father is, in some respects, like that image.

We encounter here a powerful portrayal of a colossal ocean wave that is about to crash down on to a dark, jagged rock-strewn Maine shore, under a foreboding grey sky. Here Homer seems to be attempting to give expression to the raw, indeed to the amoral, forces of nature, often surging beyond anything that we humans can imagine, even as we contemplate those very forces with awe or with fright or with both.

This is nature in itself—wild and tempestuous, sublime and overwhelming—far removed from the peaceful or even the wrenching moments of any human society. For me, this chaotic, oceanic image points us to the mysterious power of "God the Father Almighty, maker of heaven and earth," as the Apostles' Creed announces.

IV.

Second, imagine yourself standing before the large Rembrandt oil painting *Christ in the Storm on the Sea of Galilee* (1633), which I also have contemplated a number of times—before it was stolen from Boston's Isabella Stewart Gardner Museum in 1990. With my own sigh of hope for this great work's eventual return, I here want to say that I have long regarded it as inspired testimony to the mystery of the second person of the Trinity. God the Son is in some respects like the image of Jesus we can contemplate in that painting.

In this overpowering work, you can encounter the same kind of natural chaos that so transfixed Homer along the Maine coast. But here you can also be claimed by a gripping narrative that seems to emerge before your very eyes, even as you stand there with fright before that chaotic scene.

A vulnerable ensemble of fragile humans, the disciples and their teacher, Jesus, is being tossed about perilously in a small fishing boat, on bright but turgid and chaotic waves—doomed to death, they all appeared to have been. But then—and this biblical denouement isn't even suggested by Rembrandt's painting, although he surely assumed that all in his time knew the story—the very Creator-God whose powers are made manifest by those primeval waves takes hold of the narrative of that fraught experience in a remarkable way. Jesus, the Son of God, stills the waters.

When you contemplate that striking painting, you have to complete the epic story yourself. Rembrandt leaves it to us to imagine how the Creator God, now in the person of the Savior, Christ the Lord, rescues the disciples, even as the storms of chaos are threatening to drown them all.

Which means, according to the biblical narrative, which Rembrandt is depicting in part: Christ is the Lord of all things. He is the One who has arrived in the midst of our earthly chaos in order to usher in an overwhelmingly new and magnificently diverse world of cosmic harmony and peace. Countless generations of the faithful, after the apostolic era, would then fittingly come to know this Lord, who "stilled the waters," as the second person of the Trinity.

V.

Finally, contemplate with me the image of another painting by Homer, with perhaps—especially in our day, when forest fires have been rampaging everywhere—the ominous-sounding title, *Sunset Fires* (1880). I take this work to be inspired testimony to the mystery of the Creator Spirit, who, according to Genesis 1, hovers over a vast world-coming-into-being and who, according to Acts 2, comes down, as with flames, upon a distraught company of disciples who were still grieving the loss of their beloved teacher. God the Spirit is in some respects like the peace and the power that we can encounter in *Sunset Fires*.

I have never seen that painting in person, but I quickly took hold of a print the first time I could. For me, this is an unusual, even strange, Homer painting. It shows a nineteenth-century schooner, depicted in black, with full charcoaled sails, quietly, we may imagine, coursing through what appears to be a richly reddened, tranquil bay at sunset. Think of that ship as being propelled forward by the wind or the Spirit (*pneuma, spiritus*) of God. The observer can see dark forms on its deck, presumably passengers huddled there, as they are being carried peacefully forward by that schooner, and also see, nearer to the placid shore, three dark human figures in a black canoe, moving peacefully in the same direction, closer to the shoreline.

All is well with mortal human life and with tempestuous nature everywhere—that seems to be the primary message of this translucently subdued painting by Homer. I read it, more particularly, as a witness to the cosmic peace that the Spirit—recall the tongues of fire of the book of Acts, as well as the creative, hovering of the Spirit over the primeval waters in the book of Genesis—will one day bring to the whole creation, a day of peace when all the dark forces of chaos will be transfigured in eternal light; and the lamb will lie down with the lion and all things will glow in God's eternal glory.

VI.

And I thank God for disclosing to me what I now take to be these three illuminating natural images of the Trinity, consummate visual witnesses, I believe, to the glorious and unfathomable mysteries of the Father, the Son, and the Holy Spirit, one God, world without end. Amen.

XI

Praying All the Time?
Practicing the Trinity Prayer Inside and Outside

WHO WOULD EVEN *THINK* about praying all the time, never mind inside and outside? But brace yourself. That's not only possible. It can be a blessing.

Over the years I have developed a practice of prayer which opens up the promise, I believe, of what the apostle Paul called praying "without ceasing" (I Thessalonians 5:17). This way of prayer is patterned after the famous "Jesus Prayer" used by some Orthodox Christians.

I have interpreted the prayer that I practice, which I call "the Trinity Prayer," at some length for professional theologians and pastoral practitioners in my book *Before Nature: A Christian Spirituality* (2014). I have also narrated how that prayer can help to undergird a life of public discipleship in my book *EcoActivist Testament* (2022).

Here I want to introduce this short prayer and its practice to a wider audience, with the hope that since it has worked so well for me for so long, others might want to take it to heart and to practice it also—and to be blessed in the process, as I have been.

Praying All the Time?

I.

Here's a personal note, by way of introduction. I have found that this kind of prayer is especially helpful for persons like me, who, for some reason, aren't served well by trying to follow the traditional Divine Hours (praying regularly, five times a day), or who haven't figured out how to practice "daily devotions" in morning or evening or both, the way my father did all his adult life, using a small booklet provided to him by the church. For me, perhaps against much spiritual common sense, it's better to try to pray *all* the time than to depend on scheduled times—except for table grace or for the Sunday liturgy. I don't begrudge any other regular weekday times for prayer that many in our day have chosen. I just have had to find another way.

I offer a tip right at the start, too. I wear a sizeable brass pectoral cross around my neck, under my shirt, every day. That cross is a life-saver, as it were, for my prayer life. I feel it against my chest often, from morning, when I put it on, to the end of the day, when I take it off. Whenever I sense that cross on my chest, I try to say the Trinity Prayer, aloud if I'm alone, under my breath if I'm out and about. My goal is to say that prayer constantly, at some level of my consciousness—and hopefully, in so doing, to let it dwell, in some manner, in my subconscious, too. My heavy pectoral cross keeps nudging me in that direction.

Take a warning, too, at the outset. It *is* called the Trinity Prayer. But don't let that theme throw you. Don't start by thinking: Oh my God, now I'm supposed to *understand* the Trinity in order to pray without ceasing?! No, I think it's the other way around. As my sixth-grade teacher used to say, you learn by doing.

There surely *is* a way to approach the Trinity so that that central mystery of the church's faith might more and more self-consciously claim your mind as well as your heart. I write about such things in the books I mentioned above. But here my main purpose is not to help you to understand the Trinity more fully, but to help you to get going in your prayer life or to keep going with even more enthusiasm.

I'm aware, too, that I'm dealing here with a kind of spiritual conundrum. To aspire to pray constantly, on first hearing anyway, doesn't make a lot of sense. When I invite you to practice the Trinity Prayer in this constant manner, you may feel the way I did as a boy when my father laced up my first pair of ice skates and I was about to launch myself all by myself out onto the frozen pond for the first time in my life. Scared to death, I was. But I hope you will hear my father's words as meant for you, too, as you consider regularly invoking the Trinity Prayer. "Just do it," he said affectionately, as he cautiously let go of my then trembling little body.

Here's one last introductory thought. The patriarchal (male) language of the Trinity will be an obstacle for many. If it isn't so in your own mind, it should be. I spend a lot of time talking about this existential challenge in one of the books to which I've already referred, *Before Nature*. Here I simply want to affirm that, over the years, I have found it most helpful to think about "God, the Father," following theologian Jürgen Moltmann, as I've already noted, as "God, our motherly Father."

II.

This is the Trinity Prayer:

> *Lord Jesus Christ, have mercy on me.*
> *Praise Father, Son, and Holy Spirit.*
> *Come, Holy Spirit; come and reign!*

I pray each of those lines *four* times—more about this particular fourfold cadence at the end. Also I am committed to pray the whole prayer as often as I can in any single setting, morning, noon, or night, indoors or outdoors.

But the setting does make a difference. If I'm out in public, I typically won't have the kind of time I need to ponder the petitions of the Trinity Prayer when I say them. But I still will say the prayer within anyway, repeatedly, whenever I can. If I'm riding on the subway, for example, I will simply bow my head a bit and press my pectoral cross against my chest unobtrusively. Then I will start repeating the Trinity Prayer internally: and keep saying that threefold prayer in inner silence as the train rumbles noisily along.

If perchance I find myself walking along a forest path, moreover, near my family's old farmhouse in rural Maine, I will typically pause along the way to say those petitions out loud, each four times. That pause makes particular sense in those woods, for without it, were I to keep walking, I might trip over a root or be distracted by that possibility. In a related setting, behind the same old farmhouse, when I'm scything the back field and when I take a break, sitting on a light plastic chair that I've brought with me, I will inhale deeply, contemplate the mountains to the west, and start repeating the Trinity Prayer, out loud.

Or see me sitting in the sixth floor waiting room of my optometrist's office, blankly staring out the window through my increasingly blurred eyes. The waiting-room TV is blaring; hence that moment isn't conducive to much reflective prayer or reflection of any kind actually. So I try to consciously block out the noise of the TV; and then I press my pectoral cross to my chest, stare out at the blurred horizon far away, and say under my breath, right there in that optometrist's waiting room: "Lord Jesus Christ, have mercy on me... Praise Father, Son, and Holy Spirit... Come, Holy Spirit; come and reign!" And I keep saying those words within, without thinking much about it, until the attendant beckons me to come into the next room for my eye exam. I like to think of this kind of public but unobtrusive praying of the Trinity Prayer is an expression of what Dietrich Bonhoeffer once called "the secret discipline of faith."

But then there's the visible, albeit secluded, discipline of faith. I claim this energetic experience as often as I can, in settings of solitude. Imagine me, then, standing before the striking, wood-carved Latin head of Christ in my study, for example, or pausing by myself during a walk in a nearby cemetery, contemplating a large gravestone formed as a Celtic cross. If you were with me in either setting, you might see me engaged in ritual acts like these:

- When I say "Lord Jesus Christ, have mercy on me" four times, I often make the sign of the cross on my chest and end by pressing my pectoral cross into my chest.
- When I say "Praise Father, Son, and Holy Spirit" four times, I often lift up my hands, as if greeting the rising sun.
- When I say "Come, Holy Spirit; come and reign" four times, I often keep my hands uplifted and then sway left and right with each utterance, as if I were involved in some kind of ecstatic dance.

As I go through motions like these, I sometimes recall the words of the apostle Paul: that we Christians are to "present [our] bodies as a living sacrifice . . . , which is [our] spiritual worship" (Romans 12:1 NRSV).

In solitude, this kind of visible discipline—I sometimes think of this as spiritual calisthenics—often brings with it measured times for reflection, too, as I pray in a more subdued cadence. I go through the motions, for sure, but I also give myself the time to ponder the words of the Trinity Prayer along the way as I say them, often with deeper thoughts, sometimes calling to mind images such as the Father, who knows when a sparrow falls; or Jesus, the Good Shepherd carrying a lamb; or the Spirit, the Life-Giver, who was there when each of my children was born, as their mother screamed and pushed, as I waited there, trembling, to hold each one of them for a few moments.

III.

To be sure, when my children were born, that's *all* I was thinking about. The Trinity Prayer, in a sense, was far, far away from my conscious mind at those particular times. So don't be intimidated by the prospect of reflecting about the words of the Trinity Prayer every conscious moment. Sometimes you'll find yourself so deeply involved in the experiences of life that you'll be completely captivated by those experiences. Still, the Trinity Prayer can always be stirring in your soul, if not on the tip of your tongue. The point here is this: just do it, whenever you consciously can.

To recall once again my father's words as he led me onto the ice and then let go, just do it! Skate spiritually through this experience of praying the Trinity Prayer constantly, as best you can, whenever you can, saying this prayer in your heart or aloud, as often as you can. No more, for a start. You can add inner spiritual twists and turns later on, if you wish, as you become more comfortable with this kind of spiritual exercise.

And more. When you can, seek out moments of solitude to allow yourself to reflect within about the penumbra of meanings that the Trinity Prayer carries with it, when you pray. Such moments are probably the best times for the spiritual ponderings to emerge. Such moments are also, more certainly, the best times to invest your whole self, body as well as mind and spirit, in this constant praying.

When, for example, I'm alone and I start the prayer, saying *Lord Jesus Christ, have mercy on me* four times, I often stand with my hands folded and my torso slightly bowed before the crucifix that typically has claimed my attention. I usually keep my eyes open, focusing on that cross. If I'm in the woods, I can often identify a cross-like pattern in the branches of a nearby tree, to command my attention.

Then, if it is given to me, as I contemplate the shape of the crucifix before me, I begin to meditate briefly, between petitions. Typically, I think first, and many times thereafter, of my own gross inability to pray and my own egregious unworthiness to come into the presence of the crucified and risen Christ. But I come, "just as I am, without one plea." Such thoughts then can give way to sweet moments of inner peace, as I contemplate the love of God for me in Christ Jesus, my Good Shepherd, there displayed on the cross.

Confident then that I have been embraced by the mercy of the living Christ, I begin to say *Praise Father, Son, and Holy Spirit*, four times. As I pray these words out loud, as I have already indicated several times, I typically stand erect, but now with hands folded on my chest and with my eyes closed. Now and again, I will start swaying from left to right and right to left. This swaying helps me put my whole self, body, as well as mind and heart, into this act of praise.

IV.

Sometimes, with those motions of words and body in play, it is given to me to meditate about the triune God, as God is in Godself, this ineffable Mystery: (1) God as eternal Joy, (2) God as overwhelming Power, and (3) God as overflowing Love—mysteries whose depths I tentatively explore in *Before Nature*.

Prayer can be that bold: inspiring you to dream dreams and see visions of the riches and the paradoxes of the ineffable, triune God. Don't try to understand things at this moment (you can't), but do try to ponder, however briefly, what such divine mysteries might mean. Let images of the mystery of the Holy Trinity like these flow through your mind and heart, if the Spirit so moves you.

As I keep swaying from left to right and back again, eyes still closed, when I come to the third petition of the Trinity Prayer, *Come, Holy Spirit; come and reign*, I extend my arms forward and even venture to stretch upwards on my tiptoes, as some early Christians did when they prayed. Along with this, if the solitude is encompassing enough, I allow myself to imagine what some of the Spirit's works might be, as I keep swaying left and right, right and left.

Inspired by the Spirit, I believe, I allow myself to envision, as through a glass darkly, the grand history of God with the whole creation, as that history is shaped by the wisdom and the power of the Spirit, from the creative cosmic Big Bang to the catastrophic cosmic Last Hurrah—and beyond that universal cataclysm into God's infinitely rich, cosmic Eternity, the Day of the New Heavens and the New Earth.

And I celebrate in mind and heart some of the particular works of the Spirit along the way, calling forth images of the Spirit shaping and guiding and energizing all things. The Spirit—

- *shaping* our infinitely vast multigalactic universe, more particularly our gloriously blue and green planetary home with all its infinitesimal evolutionary configurations of matter, life, and mind;
- *guiding* the chaotic course of human history over the ages on planet Earth, especially lifting up the lowly and liberating the oppressed; and finally
- *energizing* the whole history of God's salvation on planet Earth, culminating in Jesus, the Messiah of biblical Israel's hopes, continuing with the historic witness of the church of Christ, and concluding, in God's good time, with the universal, cosmic dawning of the New Heavens and the New Earth, when all things will be made new and when God will be all in all.

V.

When I'm finished praying for the Spirit to reign, having precariously dreamed such dreams and eagerly dreamt such visions, I stand there in silence with my eyes wide open once more, bowing again before the particular crucifix that had commanded my attention at the outset, and I make the sign of the cross one last time on my chest, pushing my pectoral cross hard into my flesh at the very end, sometimes until it hurts.

This is one way I try to reclaim Martin Luther's deep faith that the whole history of God's self-giving love, in creation, redemption, and consummation, in addition to everything else, is accomplished for my sake—*pro me*.

VI.

Brace yourself one last time now, as I bring these explorations to a close. There's still more to practicing the Trinity Prayer, *if* you're willing to risk it. You can *sing* the whole Trinity prayer, again and again. Song may be the best way to pray this prayer or any prayer, as a matter of fact. If you're familiar with old-time hymns, moreover, you won't have any trouble singing the Trinity Prayer. I list a number of hymn tunes for various seasons of the Church Year in an appendix of my book, *Before Nature*.

Consider the tune of the "The Doxology," for example. Many American Christians, especially those who have claimed the traditions of the Protestant Reformation as their own, know this one by heart, "Old Hundredth" ("Praise God, from whom all blessings flow . . . ."). That's why I suggest getting in the habit of *repeating each of the petitions of the Trinity Prayer four times*. Old-time hymn tunes like "The Doxology" work well with that fourfold cadence.

Some years ago, during the last decade of my more than forty years in the ministry, at off hours I sometimes would find my way into the chancel of the large and beautiful neo-Gothic church building where I was then serving. Knowing that I was the only one in the building at such times, I would stand there all by myself, facing the high altar, and sing the Trinity Prayer at the top of my voice, again and again, in that cavernous holy space, bowing my head, lifting up my hands, swaying to the left and to the right.

That's the kind of resonant spiritual experience that the Trinity Prayer can offer, as you seek to discover what it can mean for you to pray constantly. I invite you to give it a try.

XII

On the Habit of Noticing
A Report from the Big Island

THE CONSTRUCT ECOLOGICAL SPIRITUALITY has by now become familiar to many, Christians and others, who are seeking to respond to our global ecojustice crisis from religious perspectives. My own explorations of the Trinity Prayer in the previous chapter and elsewhere are only one modest expression of such a global quest these days. Perhaps the most widely celebrated theological voice in this respect today is Pope Francis's, who in his encyclical *Laudato si'*, which is much on my mind in this book, has championed the importance of ecologically sensitive spiritual practices for all, for Christians especially, in this era of global emergency.[1]

To all this I want to add a suggestion. Such practices, in my experience, flourish when they are complemented by what can be called an attentiveness to the ordinary. Spirituality, as I understand it, is by no means just a matter of your interiority or mine and our inner practices more particularly. Spirituality, rightly construed, in my view, also means developing the habit of *noticing what our experience of the world around us is giving us*.

---

1. Pope Francis, *Laudato si'*, encyclical letter, May 24, 2015, https://www.vatican.va/content/dam/francesco/pdf/encyclicals/documents/papa-francesco_20150524_enciclica-laudato-si_en.pdf/.

Part Three: Spiritual Explorations

This is what I am about in this chapter, as I tell the story of what I thought was going to be an ordinary two-week vacation on the Big Island of Hawaii. Instead, it was an extraordinary adventure. I was moved to notice what that experience was giving me spiritually, in a charged way that I had not anticipated. This is the story that I want to tell you now. Come along, and see what you can see.

I.

On the morning after my wife and I arrived on the Big Island, on a half-rainy day, as we were exploring back roads near the coast in the Hilo area, we came upon an almost invisible seaside park, accessible only by a steep drop of caged-in steel stairs affixed to a towering cliff. Down at the water's edge, overlooking the waves crashing against black volcanic rocks, was a single picnic table. Sitting there in the occasional sunshine, while holding our books and reading now and again, we kept lifting up our eyes to contemplate the magnificent waves of the Pacific rolling in.

That we both had books with us was no happenstance. We carry them with us the way many other travelers carry smartphones. We take our books with us on outings, like that coastal adventure. We sometimes take them out to dinner. We regularly take them on the subway with us, on the way to concerts. Except for exceptions, we usually take them to bed with us at night. Recent generations may not understand. But, more often than not, we find those books and our conversations about them, day or night, are charged with sometimes striking discoveries. Laurel reads mostly novels, as I have already observed, and I mainly read, *mirabile dictu*, theology books.

On occasion, I will read novels, such as the one I had in hand at that little coastal park, Richard Powers's *The Overstory*. That long and complex but illuminating and deeply troubling book claimed all my reading energies during our ten-day Big Island adventure. I was fascinated, but by no means surprised, by Powers's passion for trees in particular. I immediately decided that I had found a spiritual soulmate.

Powers's novel also brought back memories of my own environmental activism during the preceding fifty years—not nearly so radical, for sure, as the protests of a number of his well-etched characters. On the other hand, if you consider theology as radical, in the sense that it's a discourse that seeks to unearth the Divine roots (*radix*) of critical historic and cosmic meanings, I've been a radical since the late 1950s, committed at every step along the way to encourage our church communities and individual Christians to get ecologically rerooted.

II.

Truth be known, though, as we began our drive around the Big Island the next day, in odd moments I kept thinking much more about environmental guilt than environmental activism or green lifestyle practices. Was it a contradiction for the two of us to have contributed to the global climate crisis so blatantly by choosing to fly to Hawaii and back? Using all those resources and producing all that pollution?

Now, I know that when I entertain such questions I can also invoke Martin Luther with some justification: "Sin boldly, trust the Lord, and rejoice in Christ." Sin boldly, eh? But at some point along the way in Hawaii I just decided not to worry about the guilt, just to live with the contradictions, and then to keep throwing myself into our trip. Was that the wisdom or the folly of old age—or both?

So it happened that early on in our journey I found myself intensely preoccupied not by tourist guilt but by what I came to think of, indeed, as the great overstory and by what that story meant for me and my wife and for our children and our grandchildren and indeed for all the creatures of the earth, now and in generations to come.

Part Three: Spiritual Explorations

III.

The trees! The trees! Especially their absence. As our trip unfolded—except for the eastern shore of the Big Island, where everything was to come to a conclusion for me—trees were often in our thoughts mainly because they were not to be seen.

That was due in large measure, it appeared to me, not to historic human use or abuse—although we met signs of that, too—but because of horrendous volcanic eruptions over the years that had buried vast swaths of green regions under black lava across much of the island. Add to that the consistently sparse rainfall in much of that region, and no wonder that the place appeared to us at times to be pervasively black or brown rather than green.

IV.

But I am getting ahead of myself. While the great overstory constantly hovered in my mind, I found myself much more consciously engaged those first days of our trip with trivialities, as the world counts such things. With the city of Hilo itself, for example. A former sugarcane outpost, Hilo seemed to me to still be very much a working-class town. Much of its coastline was replete with warehouses and loading docks and corner stores, notwithstanding obvious efforts that had been made to spruce it up with parks and upscale hotels.

At Hilo, fittingly, my wife and I stayed for a day at a small, cheap hotel. Nearby, at a restaurant that appeared to be frequented mainly by locals, we enjoyed unusually spiced drinks before dinner—the one flavored with hibiscus, the other with jalapeño. The restaurant itself was perched on posts, in anticipation of the next tsunami. But never mind that kind of calamity; probably those posts wouldn't help much, I concluded, when the next lava flow from an erupting Mauna Loa began relentlessly to flow down to the sea. Had I therefore in that restaurant stumbled onto a historic insight? Was that perhaps the story of this region of Hawaii, if not all the islands, I wondered—a richly flavored human world that was constantly vulnerable to natural disasters?

The following day we left Hilo and drove for several hours along the arid northwest coast of the Big Island, many outcroppings of which were gargantuan, some of which was an enormous sloping flatland blanketed with what were, for us, alien lava fields. Those regions appeared to us to be akin to the surface of the moon, but thoroughly black and much more jagged, at least as I recall some of the astronauts' moon photos. The regions through which we were passing were almost totally devoid of trees, often devoid even of grasses, even though they were thousands of years old.

V.

At Kailua-Kona on the western coast, which was greener, thanks to more frequent rainfall, we stayed at a small house, which we had all to ourselves, maybe ten yards from the thundering waves at high tide. One day we watched as a wiry young man emerged from the scarcely visible house adjacent to ours, hidden by trees. He easily balanced on protruding lava rocks some yards out into the turbulent waters. He carried what turned out to be a sizeable white net, which he repeatedly cast over the waves. We wondered what he was fishing for. Notwithstanding his graceful movements, he didn't seem to catch anything. Was that a parable for our times? No, I didn't want to read too much into that simple story. Sometimes fishing is—just fishing.

Another day, as we were reading on the back porch, overlooking the waves, we heard the sound of what seemed to be an extraordinary wave crashing against the dark lava shoreline wall below us. On second glance, we discovered the actual source of that strange noise. It was a massive humpback whale, maybe a quarter mile offshore, surfacing and then crashing back into the waters. On cue, a remarkable whale calf surfaced and crashed into the waters with much less resounding thunder. That wonderful duet then repeated itself three more times! I felt at that moment that something of the Divine mystery of creation had just been disclosed to me, reminiscent of Job's much more comprehensive experiences at the edge of his wilderness.

VI.

At Kailua-Kona, we also preoccupied ourselves with snorkeling, which had been the raison d'être for each of our four Hawaiian trips. The snorkeling has been my wife's passion mainly, but I—once upon a time a competitive swimmer—have eagerly paddled along with her in every instance and in every direction. The word "snorkeling," I know, sounds odd, almost as odd as the sight of us, two senior citizens, must have appeared when we entered the waters at a public park, donned in gloves and masks with air pipes, carrying flippers, she holding my hand, me balance-challenged, carefully proceeding baby step by baby step, until we finally were able to lower ourselves slowly into the thigh-deep waves, put on our flippers, and then swim out to deeper regions.

It was of course all worth it. In those deeper waters, we maneuvered effortlessly, it felt, uplifted in body and spirit by the temperate, clear water and thrilled by the sight of so many multicolored fish; we watched while they seemed casually to feed and then energetically to dart around the striking coral reefs maybe twelve feet below. It was as if we had been given a privilege, a glimpse of the fifth day of creation.

That was a powerful moment for me, quite unlike the "oceanic feeling" described by Sigmund Freud and by some mystics. Their idea is that such "oceanic" experiences drive you to *lose yourself* in the Divine, like a drop of water falling into a vast sea. On the contrary, at that moment I *found myself* in a fresh way, floating on the surface and contemplating those fish below: as one small creature among unimaginable numbers of other kinds, from the nearly infinite to the nearly infinitesimal, each one beloved by God in its own way, myself included.

VII.

While at Kailua-Kona, too, we joined a contingent of other tourists for a day on a small ship, which took us all to a secluded bay several miles to the south, a national seaside protected area, where we snorkeled and contemplated the gorgeous fish there for another couple of timeless hours. After that, on board, all the passengers and the crew enjoyed a deliciously grilled repast together. Did that mundane voyage and that simple lunch offer a kind of spiritual communion with the God who is in, with, and under and above, beyond, and beneath the worlds of human and cosmic history? For me, it did. For me, that world was charged with Divinity.

On another day at Kailua-Kona, we motored up winding roads to the top of a mountain precipice in order to find a funky cafe, where we had lunch at a window overlooking the whole coastline far below, which was bathed at that time in the sun and punctuated by the shadows of a few ominous rain clouds.

What human hands had shaped those sloping mountainside fields, I wondered, and, more recently, what had it truly cost to develop the land below, closer to the ocean, into sprawling residences for the rich and the powerful? And what other species might have lived on those slopes in times gone by? Was it possible, indeed, to hear the groaning of the whole creation in that developed setting, if one had ears to hear?

VIII.

After our stay at Kailua-Kona, we drove around the northern coast. We kept motoring higher and higher, with an ancient extinct volcano on one side and the vast shoreline extending from horizon to horizon below us. This was a region of immense grasslands, presumably cleared of trees—and of Indigenous peoples—at some time by colonizing human hands, perhaps for the sake of sugarcane production or to create flowing fields where cattle could graze. The vista at that point was overwhelming, some three thousand feet high.

Part Three: Spiritual Explorations

We then descended along a narrowing and still more winding road two thousand feet or more to what appeared to be a small tourist town, Hawi, where we enjoyed an idiosyncratic Hawaiian lunch and, with all the other tourists, dutifully applauded two middle-aged Indigenous women who were doing what were billed as traditional dances. What might I have learned from that experience had I given it any serious spiritual attention? What in particular could those women have told us, had we found some way to talk with them beyond that tourist setting?

IX.

Returning to Hilo, we took refuge in an elegant three-floor, shoreline minihotel, perched on posts, again, in view of the next tsunami. The best snorkeling we experienced on our trip was at a nearby sandy beach, thankfully not, like many of the others, full of sharp, lava rocks. The sun came out just in time for our first plunge into those nearly transparent waters. The fish there were extraordinary, some of them with colors which we had not seen before. It was their world, and I felt privileged to have had glimpses of it.

The following day, huddled together, holding firm to our single umbrella under a steady rain, we explored the shoreline in front of our inn, tiptoeing on the sometimes slippery volcanic stone flats at the edge of the ocean. At one point, we caught sight of a large sea turtle, which soon disappeared under the ledge of the rocky shoreline on which we were standing. Such turtles, we had learned, can stay under water for as much as half an hour. On a previous Hawaiian trip, to Kauai, while snorkeling, we had glided over several such creatures, none of whom seemed to pay any attention to us. It was as if they had assumed that those regions were theirs, not ours.

From that seaside base in Hilo, the next day we drove thirty-five miles to Volcano National Park and explored its many contours and precipitous sites. Somehow the fog that often shrouded us that day seemed appropriate. Every murky volcanic basin seemed to be charged with the mists of mystery. At the end of the day, as we sat in an upscale restaurant at the upper reaches of the volcano, we looked out the large windows, which were to have shown us beautiful scenic vistas, and we saw heavy grey clouds everywhere.

At that moment we might well have pondered the ambiguities and the contradictions of affluent human existence on planet Earth. By what right had we been expecting to be presented with a scenic view? Instead, we talked about the books we had been reading and we gossiped about our children and our grandchildren, along the way relishing more delicious local cuisine.

During the meal, we had a fascinating conversation with our server, whose day job was caring for a half dozen cattle. He complained about not being able to grow the vegetables he was eager to harvest, because many of them rotted in the heavy rain in that region. It was also a challenge, he said, to keep the cattle dry, which he said he needed to do for their own sakes. For sure, he was much more in tune with the meanings of that region than tourists like us were.

X.

Finally, while my wife had her snorkeling moments to keep rejuvenating her spirits, the existential high point of the trip for me was our long, contemplative visit to the Hawaii Tropical Botanical Garden not too far from Hilo, the city where we had begun our Hawaiian journey. That sun-drenched day, happily, we had the whole park almost entirely to ourselves. It was full of an unimaginable number of small, large, and gargantuan plants, from variegated orchids and spider lilies to monkeypod and African tulip and banyan trees, topped off by immense palms. The park was bounded at its lower levels by the sea itself and the rolling and the churning of the incoming waves.

A thoroughly modern human creation (1984)—containing plants and vines and trees from middle-earth regions in many settings around the globe, and doubtless also hundreds of indigenous animals that we never heard or saw, except for the songs of a few birds—this dramatically sloping forty-acre seaside garden, featuring as it did several cascading streams, was more than a park for me.

Again: The trees! The trees! As I walked along the circuitous, well-designed paths, a few of them almost too steep for me, and I looked up at the canopy high above, I called to mind some of the themes of *Overstory*. For, in this place—not without the investment of much human capital—the overstory ruled everything else.

But all the more so, inveterate student of Scriptures that I sometimes aspire to be, I thought of that place as the Garden of Eden. Laurel and I were Adam and Eve all over again, I imagined, fragile and dependent creatures who were almost totally hidden amid those astoundingly huge leafy plants and colossal trees. She at once picked up the theme of human minisculity in her own characteristic fashion, calling to mind for us the several sizeable broad-leafed tropical plants that I have collected and that I care for in our own living room back in Massachusetts. She imagined herself at that moment in that fecund Hawaiian botanical garden, she said, as some kind of inch-high humanoid walking through an overwhelmingly green effervescence of gigantic houseplants.

For me, that exquisitely alive seaside temple of towering trees, intricately variegated flowers, mysterious vines, spaciously leafed undergrowth, and crashing streams and surging ocean waves on the Big Island also brought forth feelings of sadness. What was the future of this Garden of Eden to be? Our trip happened to coincide with the weeks in 2020 when the woodlands of half of Australia, it seemed, were going up in flames.

PART FOUR

Living Ecologically

XIII

Gardening as Resistance

BACK IN THE DAY, when I served for a score of years as what we then used to call an "urban minister," I and my neighborhood clergy partners sometimes used to muse, what makes an urban church urban? The best answer at the time, for many of us was, you can tell it's an urban church when you see six feet of solid concrete between the church doorstep and the street.

Things, happily, seem to have changed. In recent decades, I've observed and I've read about numerous urban churches that have sought to transform their concrete settings, however close their front doors may still be to the streets. Among other things, some have planted gardens—wherever they could uncover some viable patch of God's good earth on their land. Some have even made neighborhood gardening—say, in a nearby vacant lot—the main point of their summer outreach ministries. Others have participated in tree-planting ministries in their neighborhoods. Still others have joined neighborhood advocacy efforts to pressure the powers that be to plant trees along their own streets or to reclaim "discarded" lots for community gardens.

An increasing number of urban congregations in all denominations are becoming "green congregations," too. That's now their identity. Some suburban congregations have claimed these trends as well, even transforming their large, well-manicured lawns into flower or vegetable gardens or places of mystery where indigenous plants can flourish on their own.

What's all this gardening about? In a sense, that's like asking, what's all our breathing about? Humans and gardens obviously belong together. Hundreds—even thousands—of scholars and poets and young romantic visionaries and wise senior citizens and earth-loving newly marrieds have written effusively about gardening over the years. If you wish, you can consult a mammoth literature on the subject, which in the West alone goes back at least as far as ancient Rome.

Why shouldn't churches be a part of this mix? Traditionally, as a matter of fact, many monasteries and cathedrals have had gardens of their own. Much has been written about those ecclesial practices, too.

I want to add a tiny footnote to this long-standing and sometimes overwhelmingly vast literature on gardening in general and on historic church practices of gardening, in particular. My theme, for our era: gardening as resistance.

I.

When you immerse yourself in the gardening life, you make a statement—or you can: *this is the way life ought to be.* You resist the thought that there's not enough food on this planet to feed all the people on this planet. You resist the thought that food scarcity is something normal. You resist the thought that global food production should be handled mainly by great corporations. For sure, in situations of food insecurity and hunger and even starvation such as we face today around the globe, we probably *do* need something like agribusinesses—well regulated, of course—as a kind of emergency response.

But beyond that kind of emergency thinking, why not also envision a totally re-formed, nature-friendly approach to producing good food for the people of the earth on a large scale, especially for the poor and the hungry? Why not also give the masses opportunities to be gardeners, whoever wants to? To that end, we of course do need to end war (!) and bring the wealthy North and the poorer South of the planet into much better balance, so that, among other things, the grain of Ukraine can regularly be shipped to where it's needed in Africa.

To end food insecurity around the earth! Enough food easily available for all! In that context, each person who wants to garden actually gardening would make a lot of sense. That, as a matter of course, can and should be our dream—and our moral marching orders all the more so.

II.

In service of that dream and those orders, you and I can also make our own statements right now, like some of the urban and suburban churches I just mentioned already have done. Capitalist agribusiness and inner city concrete are not going to rule my life. I want to live in a world where everyone who wants to can enjoy the gardening life, and where all can enjoy good, nutritious, and tasty food and also the beauty of the earth, either by working the land themselves or by joining in food cooperatives, even of global scope. And why not make it possible for all who want to grow flowers themselves to do so close to home, rather than adding to the forces of climate change by flying whole planeloads of industrial-produced flowers from Caribbean nations to be sold in New York and Boston every day?

All the more so, I want to live in a world where villages and small towns and great cities can flourish, precisely because they're rooted, directly or indirectly, in the gardening life. I want to live in a world where virtually every inner city block can have its own tree canopy. I want to live in a peaceful world, above all, where we all can blessedly say: not damn the torpedoes full speed ahead, but damn the torpedoes plant your garden bed.

I'm going to keep on gardening, therefore, as long as I can, with the Genesis 2 account of Adam and Eve in the Garden of God always in mind, because this is who we humans are, I believe, whatever else we night be. We're essentially made for the gardening life. We're essentially made to build our towns and our great cities rooted in God's fructuous earth—as garden towns and garden cities. One way of reading the Genesis 2 creation narrative is that God made *us all* to be farmers! That's why God fashioned us from and then embedded us in the earth in the first place.

Woe to those, then, who take the earth away from the people of the earth! Woe to those who master the earth and the peoples of the earth so as to prohibit everyone else, especially the poor and the oppressed, from enjoying the fruits of the earth. Woe to those, in particular, who have such a grip on the land that it's impossible for few others to have gardens of their own.

Me? I'm going to keep doing all the gardening that I can, as I've already stated, but not only as a joy forever but also and self-consciously as *an act of resistance* to the powers of death that all too often dominate the peoples of the earth. I'm going to keep scything our barley cover crop midsummers in midwestern Maine and keep turning two quadrants of our vegetable garden every fall as long as God gives me strength, because in that scything and that turning there's hope for the world.

III.

At this point, as at many others, I stand with Martin Luther—invoking a saying that I have seen quoted perhaps scores of times, by people of secular persuasion as well as by people of faith, and which I have already cited in this book. When asked what he would do if the world were coming to an end, Luther reportedly responded: "I would plant an apple tree." Whether or not he actually ever said that, we know from his whole adult life that Luther knew what it meant to resist. So, in my own modest way, hidden off in the boondocks of this world, I tend to my own gardening and—I, too, resist. And you?

XIV

Caring for Creation Isn't Enough

I BEGAN TALKING PUBLICLY about caring for creation in my first book, to which I have often referred, *Brother Earth* (1970). As the ecotheology movement grew in succeeding decades, that construct, which was never just mine by any means, found a place in the then growing discussions of ecological issues in many American denominations, especially thanks to the contributions of the Mennonite biblical scholar Theodore Hiebert (see his book *The Yahwist's Landscape*, 1996).

I.

It was no coincidence, then, that along the way the 1993 social teaching statement of the Evangelical Lutheran Church in America, *Caring for Creation*, highlighted that theme. That made compelling sense, theologically and ethically. Many other American denominations also issued similar statements of their own.

Ever since that era, I myself have made the caring-for-creation theme a central point of my typical church or college stump speeches. Here's a sample. I ask this question: "According to the Bible, why did God place Adam and Eve in the garden?" A typical answer from my audiences would be, "'To till and to keep' it." "Right," I say, "but *wrong*. That's the traditional English translation. But the biblical

Hebrew actually says, "to serve and protect" it. For Genesis, at least according to one of its creation narratives, God created human creatures, because God needed them to care for the earth!"

II.

Fast-forward now to the present: caring for creation has become a major, if not the central, theme in ecumenical ecotheology. As an aside, be it noted, another more traditional theme, stewardship of creation, has also continued to appear in some popular church discussions since the last century, as well as in the writings of a few ecotheologians, albeit with reduced frequency, and for good reason.

That stewardship theme has been critiqued by theologians like Larry Rassmussen and myself. Without going into great detail, the theological critics of stewardship hold that that construct is too managerial, too geared to the exploitation rather than the care of nature. Be that as it may, the stewardship theme has—thankfully, in my view—been fading from the discourse of most churches in recent years.

Not coincidentally, the 1993 Evangelical Lutheran Church in America statement on our earth crisis avoided using stewardship language altogether. Even more significant perhaps, Pope Francis, in his lengthy and highly influential encyclical *Laudato si'*, uses the word "stewardship" only once, by my reckoning, and that only in passing![1]

III.

My purpose here, however, is to convince you, if you need convincing, that, important as it is, biblical as it is, and preferential, I think, as it is compared to stewardship theology, the theme of caring for creation should not be allowed to stand on its own.

---

1. Pope Francis, *Laudato si'*, encyclical letter, May 24, 2015, https://www.vatican.va/content/dam/francesco/pdf/encyclicals/documents/papa-francesco_20150524_enciclica-laudato-si_en.pdf/.

Rather, caring for creation should be regarded as a *secondary* theme, due to the comprehensive crisis that we humans have brought upon ourselves and the whole earth. In a word, leaving the problematic construct of stewarding nature far behind for now, the Bible surely *does* mandate that chiefly we are to care for the earth, rather than exploit the earth. But, biblically speaking, *caring for the earth is the lesser of two good commitments*. What, then, according to Holy Scripture, is more important than caring for the earth?

Recall these fundamentals of biblical teaching. Figuratively speaking, humans no longer live in the Garden. Figuratively speaking, we live in a fallen world, outside the Garden. Do you need convincing of that? When our whole planet is now, to coin a phrase, going to hell due to humanly induced climate change?

IV.

Be reminded, then, that the construct caring for creation, according to the biblical imagination, has its primary setting in a world *before the fall*. For our fallen world, God speaks an additional Word first and foremost, not primarily a Word of blessing for humans as we rightly commit ourselves to care for creation, but primarily a Word of judgment on us humans—especially on the wealthy and the powerful around the planet—for the mess we all have made of things.

Here's an example of that Word of judgment—which is particularly sharp for someone like myself, who has invested so many energies of my professional life over the years in what I and others used to call "liturgical renewal": "Take away from me the noise of your songs; I will not listen to the melody of your harps. But let justice roll down like waters, and righteousness like an everflowing stream" (Amos 5:23–24 NRSV).

Reformulating this proclamation by Amos in terms of today's global crisis, I want to say this: however much you may preach and teach and even celebrate caring for creation as you worship, it all amounts to nothing, unless you've first responded wholeheartedly and effectively and consistently to what's happening to the poor and the dispossessed around the globe.

Did you know—of course you did—that rising global sea levels, caused mainly by historic Western industrial development and its now drastic effects of this earth's climate, first impact the lives the poor who live in the coastal regions around the world, not those, like me, who live in much more secure settings? Those rising waters are already beginning to wreak havoc on the Bangladeshes of this world. And those rising waters are at once a judgment on all of us who live affluently and securely and who have done so much, unconsciously perhaps more than consciously, to bring on climate change.

Did you know—of course you did—that the steel plants producing the material for the sleek, polluting cars some of us drive have for generations spewed poisons into the very neighborhoods where they've been located—and that these neighborhoods have often been home to low-income residents of color? All that poisonous pollution is a judgment on those of us who have lived affluently and securely, often in green belts around our cities, and who have done so much to bring on climate change, however unintentionally.

V.

Many church people, of course, have long known about such grim facts on the ground. That's why most American church bodies today—sparked by prophetic investigations already pursued by United Methodists during the last century—have claimed a relatively fresh theological construct as their own and made it a matter of first priority—*ecojustice*. Thus, already in 1993, in its statement *Caring for Creation*, the Evangelical Lutheran Church in America issued a stirring, lengthy, and carefully wrought four-part "Call to Justice," as the heart of that statement.

Caring for creation, then, has no genuine theological meaning apart from a resolute and thoroughgoing commitment to ecojustice. That's why caring for creation isn't enough. The first Word that the Lord speaks to us affluent Christians today is this: Let ecojustice roll down like an ever-flowing stream!

XV

From Lake Wobegon to the Streets of Manhattan

THE AMERICAN HUMORIST GARRISON Keillor celebrated the lives of just-plain Midwestern rural folks who lived in the now—thanks to him—well-known imaginary town of Lake Wobegon. I think that it was Keillor who once observed that while waiting at the gates of heaven the Jews will carry a shofar, the Catholics a crucifix, and the Lutherans a bowl of Jell-O. I saw signs of that Lutheran sensibility on the streets of Manhattan on Sunday, September 21, 2014, during the Peoples Climate March. I want to celebrate that sensibility here for the sake of generations yet to be born.

I.

Just about every group that I observed at that march carried its own sign or banner or flag, announcing its identity and promoting its own commitment to this good cause: the Hare Krishnas; the Unitarians; the Service Employees International Union; 350.org; the Sierra Club; the Hindus; the Women's International League for Peace and Freedom; St. John's Sunday School, Harlem; and many more.

We Lutherans carried three-by-two foot green cardboard signs, with "Climate Justice: For All of God's Creation" in large letters. In tiny print, I mean really tiny print, down in the corner of our signs: if you held the sign close to your eyes, as if you were reading a newspaper, you could identify these words: "Evangelical Lutheran Church in America." Onlookers might well have wondered, who *are* those creation-justice people with those bright green signs?

I gently chided one of the Lutheran staff workers about this, a young woman from our church's advocacy office in the nation's capital. It turned out that she had had a hand in designing those signs. "It never crossed my mind," she said, "to put 'Lutherans' in big letters. We were looking for the distinct message we wanted to convey, and we thought that 'Climate Justice for All God's Creation' was it." I agreed. Bless her. Good Lutherans always strive to announce the Truth, never to announce themselves!

On the face of it, that approach makes sense. After all, as far as I could tell, there were fewer than a hundred self-identifying Lutherans participating in that march of some 310,000 souls. And we were to make a big deal about *our* identity!? Be that as it may, I was proud (a non-Lutheran sentiment, I know) to be carrying my own modest sign. Why? Because we had it right. We had left Lake Wobegon and had headed to the streets of Manhattan. It was time to process! And that's something we knew how to do.

II.

Consider, first, the Truth of processions. The Mass for Creation that my wife and I attended at 8:45 that Sunday morning at St. Peter's Lutheran Church, Manhattan, was replete with processions: from the baptismal pool to the table, from the table, with the bread and wine, down into the midst of the people; then the people moved from the pews toward the table to meet the ministers of the Eucharist, and finally all together now we moved from the place of assembly—passing the baptismal pool and making the sign of the cross upon ourselves with the water along the way—to a meeting room, for instructions and coffee. Then we continued processing out into the streets of Manhattan.

St. Peter's does it all the more dramatically during the great Mass of the Easter Vigil. For a segment of the Scripture readings during that high liturgy, the whole congregation processes out of the sanctuary right onto the busy sidewalks of Midtown Manhattan on a Saturday night. There, led by a processional cross, vested clergy, and trumpets, the congregation sings Easter hymns as it marches to each corner of the block, from 54th Street and Lexington Avenue and back around again. At each corner the Word of God is announced, with the help of a good electric megaphone.

Let's hear it for the Gospel Procession! Call it a bowl of Jell-O, if you wish. But this is the liberating Truth—unheard amid the noise of our society as it often is—for the crowds that ply such streets at any time and for those undocumented families that pick apples in Washington State and for those nameless workers who wash the floors and change the linens in the high-rise hotels of Hong Kong and for those Inuit Lutheran parishioners whose families lived on the island of Shismaref, in Alaska, for hundreds of generations, but who have now been forced to abandon their ancestral home, for fear of being washed away by rising ocean currents.

III.

This is what I take to be the Gospel Truth of the Gospel Procession. Never mind what you see on the ground. *It's all going somewhere!* There's hope for the whole creation! There's justice, finally, for every creature! It may not look like much at that moment. What's a modest hundred, mostly waspish Lutheran marchers compared to a huge, incredibly diverse 310,000? On the other hand, what's a mere 310,000 marchers compared to the upwards of 13 million citizens who live in greater New York City? And what's a New York City committed to reducing its greenhouse gas emissions 80 percent by 2050 compared to the whole nation of India now planning to add 455 coal-fired plants for electricity in the next decade?

The point for those who identify as Lutherans in particular is this—and also for those of other Christian communions or for those who a now exploring the Christian Way: open the sanctuary doors and get that Gospel Procession out on to the streets! Never mind if others think that you're carrying Jell-O. In fact, by faith alone you're carrying the Gospel Truth. *There's hope for every creature!* That's what we've been called to announce, in the midst of all the other countless and likewise called groups and communities and organizations who also care about the good Earth and all its creatures.

I saw one sign: "Atheists for Climate Justice." I have no doubt that they were called by God to be there. For us Lutherans, I say: whatever else others might be saying or doing, even the atheists, bring your Jell-O with you to any such march. Call it our bowls of compassion.

PART FIVE

Testimony from the Arts

XVI

Gnosticism and the Earthly Vision of Vincent van Gogh

WHEN I WAS A young theological student, I was asked to participate in a group led by the then well-known Harvard professor Timothy Leary, who had already popularized the drug LSD by invoking his slogan "turn on, tune in, and drop out." In this case, he was proposing to study LSD use and mystical experiences. So, for him at that time, theology students like me were more than welcome.

I declined Leary's invitation, not on the grounds that I was troubled by what then appeared to me to be his chemical approach to spirituality (although that kind of spiritual practice did trouble me then, as now), nor because I feared putting such alien substances into my body (although I did then and still do harbor such fears), but because the meeting time of Leary's group conflicted with my regular squash game.

To this day, I remain conflicted by the kind of spirituality which came to expression in Leary's communal explorations, particularly with his use of LSD. I'm aware that some of the nation's top medical schools have in recent years set up psychedelic research centers, to investigate medical use of that drug and others like it under carefully controlled conditions. The problem back then, in my view, was the Leary worldview. For me, it had all the trademarks of what is perhaps the most dangerous kind of spirituality that we have known in the West, often called Gnosticism.

I want to explore that worldview here and then propose what for me is a compelling alternative, a vision given with the works of Vincent van Gogh. With this question in mind throughout: how is it best to—get high?

I.

For the historic Gnostic, everything depends on the inner life. Nothing external matters all that much. Indeed, a life that takes externalities—above all, the human body—seriously, according to this way of thinking, leads you nowhere and is therefore not really worth living. Gnosticism typically comes to expression in what is sometimes called a body-mind dualism, according to which our empirical existence is more or less irrelevant or even evil, and the inner spiritual core, as it isolates itself from the material world in order to commune with the world of pure spirit (or the Divine), is to be treasured above all else.

In contrast, proponents of the classical Christian tradition have regularly held that the material world of nature is created good by God and that that world indeed is the milieu in the midst of which God seeks to commune with us. This is signaled by the normative Christian teaching about the incarnation, according to which "the Word became flesh and dwelt among us" (John 1:14). It is also signified by the normative Christian affirmation that God will bring the whole creation, including the natural world, to eternal fulfilment on the day of a New Heavens and a New Earth (Revelation 21:1), not just human souls (and perhaps angels), as Gnostics have typically maintained.

Gnostic spirituality has always lurked at the door of the Christian church, and has sometimes found a way into the inner sanctum of the Christian soul. As a result, Christian theologians like Irenaeus in the second century and Augustine in the fifth century felt called upon to invest huge amounts of theological energy to identify and then to condemn this often popular spirituality.

II.

It may surprise some to learn that Gnostic thinking did not just appear in the eras of thinkers like Irenaeus and Augustine. Fast-forward to the good old USA in our own time. One does not have to maintain that Gnosticism is *the* American religion, as did the eminent American literary critic Harold Bloom, to see signs of the Gnostic spirit everywhere in American life today: especially in the free-floating quest for spirituality that is so popular in circles whose members identify with what was once called "the counter-culture." Which is where the experiments of Timothy Leary found their spiritual home.

Today such themes find expression in the thoughts of many who like to think of themselves as being "spiritual, but not religious." This apparently is a common assumption these days: that spiritual meanings which stir within the individual soul have authenticity, not so much the external and formal rites and beliefs of traditional religious communities, nor even simple earthly habits such as greeting friends at your neighborhood pub.

Visiting a Lutheran congregation once while I was on vacation, I heard the preacher say from the pulpit words like these: "I don't need to tell you about Jesus or about God. You've heard about these things for a long time. What you don't know about is—yourself. Let me introduce you to yourself—and see if we can find a way for you to *soar*, spiritually." I gave that preacher the benefit of the doubt. Probably he had no idea that he was giving voice to traditional Gnostic themes, albeit in the language of Timothy Leary.

In the meantime, while more than a few in our culture are seeking today to explore the depths and the dimensions of the inner self in ways that sometimes resemble historic Gnosticism, the external world in which we all find ourselves, if I may say so again, often appears to be going to hell. We live in a world at the edge of an international nuclear conflict, a world where climate change is threatening livable human existence almost everywhere, a world of encroaching poverty especially in the global South, a world where nations continue to make war on other nations, and where the powerful still trample on the powerless. And what really counts is my own inner spiritual life?! Mercy.

Rather than retreating from our public predicament to some protected inner sanctum, then, as historic Gnosticism and its modern offshoots have prompted us to do, I believe that we must claim the world around us anew, as the good creation that God loves in its entirety—past, present, and future—however broken and tormented this creation, in its human expressions, now appears to be.

How, then, are we to do that? How in particular are we to reaffirm the biblical promise of God's love for the whole cosmos (John 3:16), not just for a few individuals who are "in the know" (= Gnostics)?

III.

If I were to select a single anti-Gnostic Christian statement in modern times for us to claim in our quest to reaffirm God's good creation in its fullness, it would be the vision of Vincent van Gogh. Never mind his personal struggles, for now. Such things go with the human condition. Rather, think of his paintings and the theological vistas they announce.

Many know about van Gogh's glorious paintings of wheat fields, sunflowers, and that one overwhelmingly beautiful *Starry Night*. But van Gogh's own deeper religious convictions are often overlooked. The son of a Christian pastor, Vincent dedicated himself to missionary work among the poor early in his adulthood and also kept returning to biblical motifs, such as the Bread of Life, throughout his life. Many of his paintings passionately, if subliminally, celebrate God's glorious works throughout the earth and the goodness of the whole earth.

Such paintings announce that God is to be encountered here and now, in this brilliantly translucent creation, not in some other spiritual realm, whether high above or deep within. Van Gogh was, indeed, a celebrant of *the whole world of matter*, not of some other allegedly higher or deeper spiritual world. For van Gogh, passionately, matter mattered.

I see this dramatically in a number of his earliest works, particularly those rooted in his identification with the downtrodden peasants of his time, like *The Potato Eaters*. Witness in these early works his passionate empathy for impoverished coal miners in particular, in whose midst he once struggled as a lay minister of the Christian gospel of good news for the poor.

"We humans are of the good earth," I hear van Gogh saying again and again in those early works. For him, from the very beginnings of his artistic creativity to the very end, human identity is rooted in materiality, not in some ethereal realm somewhere else, accessible only by an earth-demeaning spiritual ascent or by some earth-abandoning, mystical descent into the depths of one's own interiority, drug-induced or not.

For van Gogh, the peasants working with the sun-drenched earth are telling an eternal truth, even though those peasants may in fact be succumbing to early deaths due to their poverty. Van Gogh, I believe, was always a faithful celebrant of the earth, even in the darkest of times. Witness his early drawing of peasant shoes, which in their solitary blackness tell a story of what's real in human life, in particular as the poor experience it. I, for one, contemplating those shoes, can hear the groaning of the whole creation.

We can laud van Gogh's artistic gifts for many reasons, but this, in our time, when Gnosticism is such a clear and present spiritual danger, is perhaps the most important of them all. Van Gogh passionately loved the earth and the people who walked most truly on the earth.

IV.

Later in his life, van Gogh never lost touch with the world of *The Potato Eaters*, even as he was also overcome by the invitation of his Savior, who had ministered to the poor, Jesus, to "Behold the lilies of the field . . ." Notwithstanding all of van Gogh's personal struggles, this man of the earth was to become perhaps the greatest witness in the modern West to *beholding*, as he celebrated the gorgeous flowers of the fields and the glorious, sun-drenched wheat fields that he considered to be gifts of the very God who first called him to minister to the coal miners of this world.

Whether van Gogh ever self-consciously thought about the motifs in *The Potato Eaters* on the one hand and of the brilliant wheat fields on the other as corresponding to the biblical themes of death and resurrection can be left an open question. But, subliminally or unconsciously, motifs of death and resurrection appear to have moved him deeply.

Remarkably, I believe, those very motifs came together organically for him in what is now widely regarded as his greatest—and in fact his last—painting, *Wheatfield with Crows* (1890). Numerous interpreters, particularly those of a secular persuasion, consider that painting to be one horrendous, final expression of *despair*, signified by the dramatic presence of the crows, traditionally the archetypical symbols of death. After all, was not van Gogh about to commit suicide? Why wouldn't he foreshadow that kind of wrenching death in his last painting, unconsciously if not consciously?

But a more generous reading of that painting is also possible and, I believe, more resonant with van Gogh's lifelong spiritual pilgrimage, which began with the dark images of *The Potato Eaters* and then carried him to and through the bright and living hopes of his wheat field paintings. *Wheatfield with Crows*, it appears to me, gives sober but brilliant testimony to the classical faith of the church—to death and resurrection—however subliminally such themes might have stirred in van Gogh's conscious mind.

The black hues etched into that painting's sky and the images of the many black crows in flight themselves announce the powers of death, of the cross—or so that painting speaks to me. Van Gogh had been pondering death deeply for some time before the *Wheatfield with Crows* painting. Death, indeed, had become a kind of fixation for him in his series of cypress paintings. Those trees, surely for him and also for many of his contemporaries, stood as harbingers of death and were often associated with cemeteries. The images of the crows in his last great painting likewise gave expression to the same themes of death and dying.

On the other hand, that central country lane, running through that golden wheat field, from the foreground to the horizon, depicts, it appears to me, the way to eternal life. All this is embraced by that pervasive motif of van Gogh, the aforementioned glorious wheat fields, which, surely, for him—the preacher's son and the witness who had spent many of his early years as a freelance evangelist and preacher—proclaim the Bread of Life, the sacrament of salvation.

V.

Wheatfield with Crows. Could this extraordinary nineteenth-century painting of death and resurrection be the word of promise that our twenty-first-century world of all too pervasive cosmic despair needs to encounter and to celebrate all over again—or perhaps for the first time? Could this wrenching yet profoundly hopeful visual testimony to the ultimate redemption of matter help us today to triumph over any spirituality that demeans the world of nature and our bodies in particular?

Contemplating *Wheatfield with Crows*, I, for one, am always left with hope for the whole world of nature, both in its terrestrial and its cosmic expressions, and, still more, with hope for this earth's Potato Eaters, whom van Gogh never forgot. The way to eternal salvation is intended first and foremost for the people of the earth, according to van Gogh's angle of vision. The blessings of a gloriously renewed natural world, offering the Bread of Life to all in a gloriously charged world of nature, beyond the ravages of personal death and cosmic despair—that was van Gogh's final vision.

Thank you, then, dear Vincent, for showing us so brilliantly how to overcome the voracious claims of Gnosticism. Your works give me a down-to-earth high, which I can never fully understand, but which constantly claims my soul.

XVII

J. M. W. Turner's *Slave Ship*, Nature, and Having Eyes to See

THE TWENTIETH-CENTURY GERMAN PLAYWRIGHT Berthold Brecht once said something like this: "When I see a beautiful Mediterranean fishing village, with its small white houses etched against the deep blue waters, under the luminescent rays of the brilliant sun, I see the torn fishing nets." Brecht was not one to be taken in by romantic vistas. He always saw first the struggles of the poor of this world—perhaps even the struggles of the creatures of nature. Brecht, I believe, had eyes to see.

So did J. M. W. Turner, with no less insight than Brecht. Witness especially his widely hailed 1840 painting called *Slave Ship (Slavers Throwing Overboard the Dead and Dying, Typhoon Coming On)*. Here the sublime and the horrible collide. Here beauties of nature and murderous human perpetrations merge in brilliant but hellish hues.

I.

This is the backstory of that Turner painting. He had heard the account of a slave ship whose masters had thrown numbers of the enslaved overboard, apparently to make it possible for those masters, later, to collect insurance on "property lost at sea." Turner painted that story as a seascape in 1840—including miniscule images of many Africans who had been thrown overboard in chains into the dark waters of death.

For Turner, the occasion of the painting was to mark a major antislavery conference in London that very year. He thereby laid claim to the translucent and sometimes alien glories of nature and to the brutalities and the torments of human existence within one frame, like few other painters have been able to do. He, indeed, had eyes to see.

II.

Not so for many other painters of his era, among them the much celebrated members of the Hudson River school—whose works I, for one, have often sought out in museums. Surely many of their paintings are beautiful—mainly massive, often gorgeous, landscapes. But, may I say, against long-standing American celebrations of those grand works: such paintings often are not just luminescent; they also are illusory.

That, for example, is how I read the great 1844 painting by the founder of the Hudson River school, Thomas Cole, *Frenchman's Bay, Mount Desert Island, Maine*. Executed at about the same time as Turner's *Slave Ship* painting, *Frenchman's Bay* displays dramatic tidal surges running along steep and jagged cliffs. But there are no signs of human anguish in this painting. Those tidal surges seem harmonious, too, almost as if the painting itself had been intended to be a still life. For Cole, nature appears to be first and foremost a pristine and dramatic, but self-contained world of its own. No suggestion of torn fishing nets here. Did Cole have eyes to see?

III.

The painters of the Hudson River school, I believe, generally presupposed what I called in my first book, *Brother Earth* (1970), following the historian Perry Miller, the schizophrenia of the

American mind. That fractured vision of reality shows us two worlds of experience, which were often pitted against each other: Nature and Civilization.

The first, whose chief representative I have taken to be Henry David Thoreau, was a world of pristine if agitated glory that was alleged to offer solace to broken or weary souls. The second, whose chief representative I have taken to be a later figure, Henry Ford, was a world of stark urban struggle, between the allegedly visionary lords of industry and the allegedly mindless masses of the poor.

Faced with this kind of schizoid cultural choice between Nature and Civilization, numerous American painters, above all the Hudson River school, celebrated wilderness vistas. They announced, visually, that the nation could best find healing by a "return to nature."

The point here is not that painters of the Hudson River school never depicted any kind of human presence in nature. They sometimes did. The point rather is that in addition to everything else that their art highlighted, they consciously or unconsciously presupposed a consistent social agenda: to radically minimize the struggles of human life in contrast to the grandeur of nature.

In a word, they turned their backs on New York City and dramatized the vistas of that city's major river upstream, as if the traumas of urban existence—poverty, slavery and its aftermath, and any kind of class struggle—did not exist. Nor were these painters much interested in what might be thought of as the positive values of urban life in that era, such as mutually supportive neighborhoods, religious associations, social clubs, workers' cooperatives, and some vision of a better life for the poor one day. The Hudson River school represented a movement of ideological escape at least as much as an aesthetic vision of natural glory. Its artists never really saw the torn fishing nets.

IV.

Thoughts like these pulsated in my mind early in 2022 when I joined many other New Englanders in making a pilgrimage to the

J. M. W. Turner's Slave Ship, Nature, and Having Eyes to See

Museum of Fine Arts (MFA) in Boston to contemplate its stunning exhibit of dozens of paintings by J. M. W. Turner. Indeed, as I paused to contemplate numerous brilliant canvases by that great nineteenth-century British artist, I knew where I was going—to contemplate one more time his vision of *The Slave Ship*.

Since that painting is owned by the MFA, I had seen it at different times, as an undergraduate and then as doctoral candidate in theology: and now as a retired octogenarian pastor and ecotheologian. Permit me then this perhaps odd-sounding observation, as one long-standing student of that work by Turner: every time I have stationed myself in front of that amazingly colored painting, this time being no exception, I have experienced *existential dread*, especially as one who has devoted so much of his life thinking about and encountering the world of nature.

How can one even *think* about a slave ship, never mind contemplate its agonies etched in the brilliant colors of its natural milieu? Once you have seen that painting by Turner, can you ever contemplate the majesties of nature again in the way that many members of the Hudson River school routinely did? Turner, I believe, surely had eyes to see. He showed us the overwhelming beauties and the wrenching tragedies of our world in one vision of a certain ship sailing away through those surging seas of color.

V.

When I came home from the Turner exhibit, I kept asking myself: do I really have eyes to see? More particularly, do I have eyes to see the glories—and even at times, the agonies—of nature in a way that does not blind me to the excruciating realities of that Slave Ship?

XVIII

Titian
Women, Myth, Power—and Nature

OF COURSE MY WIFE and I had to see the much-heralded exhibit at Boston's Gardner Museum in the fall of 2021, *Titian—Women, Myth, and Power*. For me, that exhibit turned out to be about Women, Myth, Power—and Nature. But more about that in a moment.

The exhibit itself was an amazing event. For the first time in five hundred years (!) this preeminent Renaissance artist's series of six monumental paintings on mythological themes from classical antiquity had all been gathered in the same room. This was the exhibit's only showing in the US, along with stops in London and Madrid.

Titian created these grand paintings between 1551 and 1562 for King Philip II of Spain. All of them featured fulsome naked women, with titles like *The Rape of Europa* and *Venus and Adonis*. Especially in Boston, where two confident women were at that very time competing for the office of mayor, this exhibit was fittingly about—"women and power." All the more so, in view of countless centuries of male violence directed against women, the Gardner exhibit had to tell *that* story in so many words, whatever other aesthetic values it might have sought to highlight more visually.

How could anyone not cringe upon seeing those huge images of—implied—male power!? That the *Boston Globe*'s—male—reviewer did not even allude to the issues of women and male power, I found sobering, but not surprising.

I.

For me, that exhibit was a wrenching experience. What about the male gaze, Paul? How much has your own consciousness, not to speak of your unconscious, been distorted and contorted by that gaze? You began your vocational trajectory as the male chaplain of a women's institution, Wellesley College.

You once took your small children to witness a traditional senior-year event at that institution: to see members of the senior class, wearing their graduation hats and robes, rolling Hula-Hoops as fast as they could in a race to see who might win, and you knew in confidence from one of your students ahead of time that—it being the era of the '60s, after all—several of those students were going to throw off their graduation robes to reveal their naked selves halfway through the race. It was called "streaking" in those days. Whatever else you were doing there, Paul, didn't you go there to gaze?

As a male in your eighties, moreover, who is still struggling to outgrow your adolescence, can you answer this question, notwithstanding your long-standing public support for women's liberation and the more than fifty years you have invested in what has turned out to be a genuinely humane marital partnership? What did you really see when you contemplated those paintings by the great Titian?

Be that as it may, no one who has an ounce of objectivity in their soul can rightfully deny that we still live in what many women in our era have consciously or unconsciously thought of as a "rape culture." This wasn't just Philip II of Spain's problem, nor only the problem of eager sycophants like Titian. Coincidentally, the night before our visit to the Titian exhibit, my wife and I had seen the film *The Last Duel*, featuring Matt Damon and Ben

Affleck—which, in medieval guise, was all about male violence in general and the rape of women in particular. This stuff still sells. And it still tells.

II.

While I keep pondering it all, with sadness and even dread, I now come to the main point of this discussion. All of it—it's *not* about art! Or not necessarily so. Art, ironically perhaps, isn't what comes to my mind as I reflect about those paintings. They're all about the theme of rape, yes, but in this case they're also about *the rape of the earth and the forgotten peoples of the earth*—a theme I learned many years ago, starkly, from ecofeminist theologians. In the historic West, if not elsewhere, *nature* has often been feminized—think "Mother Nature." And nature has routinely and often self-righteously been violated by the powerful, most of them men.

To be sure, Titian has on occasion been celebrated for his attention to nature, and perhaps rightly so. One scholar, Antonio Mazzotta, has argued indeed that Titian's first great achievement as a painter was to depict nature with a new vitality, this under the influence of Bellini (whom I myself once modestly championed for his great painting of Saint Francis).

And more. Titian apparently projected his celebrations of nature under the influence of yet another famous artist, the German master Albrecht Dürer. The latter's works, which often featured naturalistic images of plants, animals, and landscapes more generally, were hugely popular in Venice early in the sixteenth century, according to Mazzotta.

But I didn't see any thoroughgoing influence of Dürer in the six paintings by Titian at the Gardner. Dürer was interested in nature in itself, as a world with its own meanings. An etching by Dürer of a rabbit, for example, tells the story of that creature's own integrity in the greater scheme of things.

In contrast, those paintings by Titian regularly depicted nature as—background. It was a richly hued background, to be sure. But to me, nature in those paintings seemed to be more akin to its representations in some medieval and late-medieval paintings, where one *can* see that milieu of God's creation, often in variegated colors, but only through a window next to or behind the Virgin.

The world of nature in such Renaissance and medieval paintings is, as it were, boxed in. There, to be sure, nature is often strikingly embellished with colors that sometimes have prompted me to think of works by Turner. But nature is still defined by the dynamics of *human* meaning, however elegantly or spiritually that meaning might have been envisioned. So for Titian, in these particular paintings at least, the human mythos defines everything else. For Titian, the human action in the foreground is the whole point of each of these paintings. The natural background is precisely that, merely background.

III.

And in fact as well as in art, that mythos of the human for many of Titian's contemporaries was also a mythos of violence—not only toward women but also toward subjugated peoples more generally and indeed toward the earth itself. Philip II stood for Empire. For him, the world was there for the taking. The world was there to be exploited for the sake of the powerful, particularly the dominant males. Nature, however beautiful it might be in the gaze of the lords of this world, was most fundamentally for them a cornucopia of resources, such as gold or spices or mahogany or slaves—or beautiful women.

Given this colonizing vision of the world that Philip II took for granted, could the global ravages by modern capitalism, in every corner of the earth, be far behind? Rape culture, it was soon to be revealed, plied its ravaging and raging not only against women but also against the poor of the earth and the earth itself.

That is the commentary I want to add to the truths about women, violence, and power that are so dramatically evident, for those who have eyes to see, in those six magnificent paintings by Titian. When you see the six naked women, you see what was to become the wrenching future of the whole earth. Those paintings were about women, myth, power—*and* nature.

PART SIX

Faith's Cosmic Vision

XIX

Who Then Is This?
From "Jesus Loves Me" to "the Cosmic Christ"

As a college chaplain for many years, I would on occasion talk with students who grew up in the church about what they learned about Jesus in their earliest years. Once a student who was fully at ease with her faith started smiling and then began humming the old Sunday school tune, and even singing the words, "Jesus loves me, this I know, for the Bible tells me so."

"Cool," I responded. And I joined in, as we both tried to recall all the words. We got quite boisterous. I've always wondered whether the office secretary, who was sitting on the other side of the door, overheard us and started humming along with us.

Once another very pious student asked me, checking me out, I suppose: "Is Jesus your personal Lord and Savior?" I said, "Sure, and much more." And I asked her—perhaps I shocked her—whether she knew the Elvis Presley song about putting her hand in the hand of the man who stilled the waters. That was a reference, of course, to the Gospel of Mark's narrative about Jesus calming stormy waters on the Sea of Galilee and thus rescuing his disciples, who were in a boat on those tumultuous waves, being tossed around, their very lives in danger.

On occasion, when a student would come to me to talk about her doubts, I would refer to both those songs. At some point, I might say this: "Let's imagine that there's something real going on in 'Jesus Loves Me' and 'Put Your Hand in the Hand.' Not that you *have* to believe any of this stuff. But should you wish to, this is big stuff, as big as you and me and the whole universe."

Of course, such conversations were as a matter of course fraught with questions about the viability of such biblical narratives for us, living as we were then, as now, in a world of nature that was thoroughly—but not exclusively, I always stressed—defined by the natural sciences. I mean, Jesus loving me is one thing, but Jesus calming the stormy waters of the Sea of Galilee is something entirely different, at least for anyone who's ever taken Physics 101.

Here I want to revisit that kind of discussion. In an era when the very future of human life on planet Earth is in question due to climate change, pervasive social injustice, and related threats to the biosphere, and when the universe we live in, as depicted by cosmological physics, is often for us unimaginably foreboding, hugely complex, and apparently destined for some kind of colossal "heat death," according to the second law of thermodynamics, we owe ourselves this much as people who find ourselves claimed in some manner by the Christian faith, or who at least now and then as people who aspire to be so claimed: we owe it to ourselves to find some way to affirm those New Testament texts that announce that Jesus is not just the Lover of our souls but also the Lover of the earth and indeed of the whole creation—that he's the *Cosmic Christ*. How can we talk about this?

I.

I want to begin with a memory of Krister Stendahl, the dean of Harvard Divinity School many years ago, during the same era when I was a student there. Stendahl, a New Testament scholar, often reflected about "the peril of modernizing Jesus." The challenge, he was wont to say, is to see Jesus in his often, to us, strange historical setting rather than to picture him mainly in our own image.

Stendahl would then sometimes tell the—hopefully concocted—story of a famous New Testament historian who researched the life of Jesus and wrote much about it. That very scholar is alleged to have looked down into a well one time and, seeing his own face reflected in the water at the bottom, said: "That's Jesus."

The challenge, obviously, is to see Jesus, as best we can, not only as someone who may be like us, but also as someone who may be very strange to us. That's precisely the kind of view of Jesus that I want to highlight here, Jesus as—the Cosmic Christ. To this end, let me call to mind more familiar approaches to Jesus, as a backdrop for these explorations.

II.

To begin, there's *Jesus the Friend*. According to the Gospel of John (15:15), Jesus called his disciples friends. I learned to sing "What a Friend We Have in Jesus!" in Sunday school.

In those days, that was a sentimentalizing image for many. But today, I imagine, for you and for me, it's a poignant thought. Or it can be. I mean, when everybody's "friending" everybody else in the world online, who doesn't need a *real* friend?

Second, there's *Jesus the Teacher*. That's how the disciples addressed Jesus on the Sea of Galilee when their boat was being tossed about by treacherous waves and their very lives were at stake; they addressed him as teacher.

The twentieth-century Lutheran theologian and martyr Dietrich Bonhoeffer took this image with profound seriousness. Bonhoeffer juxtaposed Jesus the authoritative teacher—"Blessed are the peacemakers"—over against the warmongering propaganda of Hitler. And Bonhoeffer lost his life in the process. That, for Bonhoeffer, was the cost of his discipleship, being a thoroughly committed follower of that Teacher.

Third, there's *Jesus the Savior*. Never mind now the hymn that I learned as a child and still love—"Beautiful Savior." If you've ever done any traveling in Europe, visiting the cathedrals of France, say, you'll have encountered crucifixes everywhere, in and around those magnificent structures. Those stark crucifixes are much closer to the popular, historic imagination in such lands than is the hymn "Beautiful Savior." But what's going on here? Why all those crosses?

Here's one thought. In our own era, Dorothy Day went to Mass every day, mostly in New York City. In the process, she *adored* the cross, as *the* sign, for her, of her eternal salvation. And she took that cross onto her own frail shoulders as a witness to the suffering love of God for this world of strife and hunger.

A broken woman in some ways, one who nevertheless is probably going to become an official saint one of these days, Dorothy Day was not only one who adored the cross. She also was a radical Christian pacifist and a champion of the poor. But Dorothy Day begged her many followers not to emulate *her*, but to emulate the Savior on the cross. Dorothy Day's reverence for the cross held her remarkable life together.

Jesus the Friend. Jesus the Teacher. Jesus the Savior. Those are the images of Jesus that are sometimes popularized, but which are biblical to the core. That's the Jesus whom I was taught to know and to love by my parents and Sunday school teachers and pastors and a whole range of other faithful witnesses. I imagine that most people today who were reared in the church and most new Christians too probably resonate with these images of Jesus, even as most at one time or another also have struggled to make sense of it all.

III.

Then there's the Jesus whom you don't know. Or the Jesus, who may seem exceedingly strange to you, even alien. You look down into the well, and you see an image that you can't even recognize. I could call this Jesus "the Lord." But that word itself might be *too* familiar just by itself, even familiar to the point of having lost its meaning.

"My Lord!" we sometimes exclaim, when we've been taken aback. Say, when you're about the cross the street, and a car runs a red light. So you come to an abrupt halt. In this case, saying "My Lord" has all the emotional traction of "Oops!," which you may utter when you've inadvertently splashed coffee on the tablecloth.

The word "Lord" is problematic for other reasons, too, above all because most "lords," historically speaking, have been men of power who "lorded it over" others. So we are best advised, I think, to set that word aside, or to use it only very sparingly, when we talk publicly about Jesus today. Jesus obviously never lorded it over anybody.

Hence I want to take you a step further. According to the New Testament—especially the Letter to the Colossians, usually attributed, rightly I believe, to Paul—and according to a variety of voices in the historic church, most recently the American Lutheran twentieth-century theological pioneer Joseph Sittler, according to all these witnesses, the risen Jesus Christ, who's overflowing with the Spirit, is *the One who embraces all things*—not just humans. He is *the Cosmic Christ*, whose Divine power holds all creatures in the universe together and who draws all of them, like a shepherd leading a flock, into a new relationship of fulfilment in God, eternally.

IV.

The Cosmic Christ? According to biblical faith? Yes. What could this possibly mean? In response, I want to take you to what I believe is the biblical heart of the matter.

Consider first the voice of the Letter to the Colossians, with reference to the ministry of Jesus Christ to and for all things, the whole cosmos. This is that letter's powerful testimony to the Cosmic Christ:

> He is the image of the invisible God . . . for in him all things were created, in heaven and on earth, visible and invisible . . . —all things were created through him and for him. He is before all things, and in him all things hold together. (Colossians 1:15–17 RSV)

From this biblical angle of vision, we can say that Jesus, whom we call Christ, is *the majestic Divine center of the whole universe.* The eminent twentieth-century Catholic thinker, the Jesuit paleontologist Pierre Teilhard de Chardin, even envisioned the risen Christ as a kind of universal divine *magnet,* who draws *all things* together and then forward on into Eternity, for the sake of their ultimate salvation.

V.

I believe that the biblical text from the Gospel of Mark about the disciples and Jesus being tossed about by huge waves—and Jesus reigning supreme over those waves—opens up the possibility of such cosmic visions, when it concludes its narrative of "the man who stilled the waters" with this question: "Who then is this, that even the wind and the sea obey him?" (Mark 4:41 RSV).

From Mark's perspective, for sure, the ministry of Jesus *does* have cosmic significance. Mark's testimony is more indirect than that of the Letter to the Colossians, where we encounter Christ as the uniting center of all things. But Mark's testimony to the Christ who stills the tumultuous waters is forceful in its own way. In light of such witnesses, we can fittingly think of Jesus, in addition to having many other meanings, as *the* center, as *the* ultimate magnet, of all things, that is, of the whole universe.

Some years ago, I had the great privilege of visiting several of the famous "painted monasteries" of Romania. My son and his family had been living in that country at the time, so that that trip was a natural. For my son and his wife, my brother, my wife, and me—not so much for my son's two young boys—those were exquisite holy sites, from the fifteenth and sixteenth centuries: small monastic chapels painted inside with gorgeously colored icons of the saints and also outside over many of those chapels' white walls.

One thing that all those monastic churches had in common was this—inside. If you've ever visited an Orthodox church, you won't be surprised. In the central dome of all those churches, you can look up and be able to contemplate the image of that Icon of icons, the face of the cosmic Christ, the Ruler of the universe, the *Cosmokrator*. Orthodox churches all over the world have thus kept this ancient biblical witness to Jesus alive: "Who then is this, that even the wind and the sea obey him?"

VI.

Now, *our* culture in the West today has been permeated by a certain kind scientific rationality, which presupposes that the Bible might *talk* about so-called mysteries; but that, of course, everybody knows that miracles, in particular, *can't* happen. Like Jesus' stilling of the waters. Some kind of miracle story, eh? So much for that.

Miracles can't happen? In *our* world? Where black holes swallow whole galaxies, and electrons on one side of the universe are entangled with electrons on the other side of the universe? Nobody knows how, at least for now. Miracles can't happen in our world? Where trees in the forest seem, as it were, to talk to one another through their root systems and sometimes even appear to look out for each other? In *this* world, miracles can't happen? Then there's the transcending beauty of the lilies of the field. Is there anything else in the whole universe more glorious than these flowers? Aren't they, in the best sense of the word, miraculous?

As Martin Luther once said, miracles happen all over the place—not an exact quote. This is Luther's own language: if you truly understood a grain of wheat, you'd die of wonder. Again, Luther: the miracles in a single apple tree are greater than the sacrament of the altar. For Luther, *everything* in nature can be regarded as a miracle, when contemplated with the eyes of faith.

Which is to suggest that whatever actually happened when Jesus reportedly stilled the waters, *something amazing* did happen. And it was overpowering and incomprehensible, miraculous in its own way, for the disciples. Later, we can imagine, each of the disciples told his friends and neighbors about it. We can imagine each disciple casting the story in terms of his own experience, making for what might well have been a cacophony of testimony to that single, extraordinary event.

VII.

Of course, the disciples saw their world through the lenses of their own cultural traditions—just the way you and I see our world through the lenses of our particular cultural traditions, ours profoundly shaped by the modern natural sciences. This is surely an important interpretive fact, which I, for one, want to celebrate, rather than be embarrassed by.

The disciples, as believing first-century Jews, presupposed the language of faith that had been bequeathed to them by their forebears. We can be drawn into that apostolic experience, imaginatively, I believe, as we hear various biblical narratives. The church helps us to do that, as a matter of fact, through its lectionary.

That's one reason, I think, why the story of Jesus stilling the waters, when read aloud on a given Sunday, is accompanied by other particular readings—first, from the book of Job. God, for Job, is the majestic ruler of the whole creation. No surprise, then, that one of my favorite ecoactivists, Bill McKibben, found himself driven to write a moving book about Job![1]

These are words from God, according to Job, familiar words for some: "Where were you when I laid the foundation of the earth? Tell me, if you have understanding . . . [Was it I who] shut in the sea with doors when it burst out from the womb?—when I made the clouds its garment, and thick darkness its swaddling [clothes] . . . , and [who] said [to the chaotic waters], 'Thus far shall you come, and no farther, and here shall your proud waves be stopped'?" (Job 38:4–11 NRSV)

The Psalms are full of such language too—for example, this, which is read along with the text from Job on the same day: "[The people] saw the works of the LORD and his wondrous works in the deep. For he commanded and raised the stormy wind, which

---

1. Bill McKibben, *The Comforting Whirlwind: God, Job, and the Scale of Creation* (Cambridge, MA: Cowley, 2005).

lifted up the waves of the sea. They mounted up to heaven, they went down to the depths . . . Then [the people] cried to the LORD in their trouble, and he brought them out from their distress; he made the storm be still, and the waves of the sea were hushed" (Psalm 107:24–29 NRSV).

The vision of Jesus exuding power enough to calm the raging waters of the Sea of Galilee resonates with such ancient themes, from Job and the Psalms. The disciples lived in *that* kind of strange—to us—world. The world as they experienced it was charged with the presence and the power of the God confessed by their forebears.

For them it then was natural, as it were, to imagine that Jesus, somehow, some way, inexplicably embodied the powers of the Creator God witnessed to in the Old Testament, there at the Sea of Galilee.

Then there's you and me. Do *we* know how the events narrated in this Gospel story happened? For sure we don't. But the story surely reflects what we do know about such waters.

VIII.

To this very day, windstorms can arise on the Sea of Galilee with a kind of terrible ferocity. Gusts charge down narrow valleys and hit the waters with huge force. Storms on the Sea of Galilee, in Jesus' time, like ours, must have been fearful to the point of terror. But, all of a sudden, too, there can be a charged—calm.

I, for one, can resonate. One summer, when I was fifteen, I and a friend were out in a canoe on Lake George in upstate New York. And we weren't paying attention, of course. We should have noticed the dark clouds gathering. In no time, huge swells were all around our canoe, lightning was flashing, thunder was resounding, and we had to frantically paddle to a little island in the middle of the lake, lest our canoe be swamped. There, soaked and shivering, we waited for the storm to pass. Of course we were scared to death. For us, it was a miracle: we had escaped alive!

But keep this in mind. The point of the *biblical* story of Jesus stilling the waters is not the physics, not the meteorology, not even the psychology of the situation, but *the identity* of Jesus: "Who then is this, that even the wind and the sea obey him?" Could this friend, this teacher, this savior, also be one with the Creator, the ruler of the whole universe?

IX.

Who then *is* this?

An English New Testament scholar once wrote a book with the title *Your God is Too Small*.[2]

Is your *Jesus* too small? If so, enlarge your image of Jesus and take a deep dive into the mystery of his identity. Imagine yourself, for example, participating in the Sunday Eucharist of a nearby congregation. Imagine yourself coming forward to receive the bread and the wine, in order to live out and join in the faith that the church proclaims. Imagine yourself, then, being encountered invisibly by the living Christ in, with, and under the elements offered to you and in fellowship with the people gathered there as the body of Christ.

Then, as you see yourself returning to your pew, imagine yourself also dreaming dreams and seeing visions in the depths of your soul—of Jesus, the risen and exalted Christ. See yourself being caught up in such a vision: that the very Christ who comes to you in the Eucharist, personally and intimately in the midst of that fellowship, is indeed your Friend, your Teacher, and your Savior, who died for you on the cross.

But also see yourself imaging that this very Christ is your cosmic Mother, if I may say so, the *Cosmocrator* of the whole universe. Imagine that all things in the universe are held together in this Christ, that he constantly draws all things into his cosmic embrace, from the very beginning of the universe to its ending, from its creation to its final fulfilment in God, when God will be all in

---

2. J. B. Phillips, *Your God Is Too Small* (London: Epworth, 1952).

all: Christ, the ruler and the friend and the savior of all creatures, comprehending the smallest of particles and the largest of galaxies, all the black holes, and everything else.

Hence, it can be given to us, with the eyes of faith, in Pope Francis's words in *Laudato Si'* (887), to see all creatures, large and small and in between, "no longer . . . under a merely natural guise, because the risen One is mysteriously holding them to himself and directing them towards fullness as their end. The very flowers of the field and the birds which his human eyes contemplated and admired are now imbued with his radiant presence."[3]

X.

This is the kind of cosmic vision to which Colossians, like the Gospel of Mark, but more explicitly, gives expression. Jesus Christ was there—as God-with-all-things—when all things came into being and he now is shepherding all things in their infinite and infinitesimal temporal courses. Jesus Christ is, as it were, the Divine Nurturer of all creatures, large and small, in their cosmic becoming, from Alpha to Omega.

See all things, then, finding their final fulfilment in his eternal embrace, when God will one day usher in the era of the New Heavens and the New Earth. This is something of the profound mystery of Jesus' identity—as the cosmic Christ—according to the New Testament.

If you're not yet ready to let your mind and heart soar in this way as you think about Jesus Christ, dreaming dreams and seeing visions—and it *is* a lot—I encourage you at least to meditate on this question, again and again: "Who then is this, that even the wind and the sea obey him?" Amen.

---

3. Pope Francis, *Laudato si'*, encyclical letter, May 24, 2015, https://www.vatican.va/content/dam/francesco/pdf/encyclicals/documents/papa-francesco_20150524_enciclica-laudato-si_en.pdf/.

Other Books by the Author

Brother Earth: Nature, God, and Ecology in a Time of Crisis. New York: Nelson, 1970.
The Travail of Nature: The Ambiguous Ecological Promise of Christian Theology. Philadelphia: Fortress, 1985.
South African Testament: From Personal Encounter to Theological Challenge. Grand Rapids: Eerdmans, 1987.
Nature Reborn: The Ecological and Cosmic Promise of Christian Theology. Theology and the Sciences. Minneapolis: Fortress, 2000.
Ritualizing Nature: Renewing Christian Liturgy in a Time of Crisis. Theology and the Sciences. Minneapolis: Fortress, 2008.
Before Nature: A Christian Spirituality. Minneapolis: Fortress, 2014.
Behold the Lilies: Jesus and the Contemplation of Nature—A Primer. Eugene, OR: Cascade Books, 2017.
Celebrating Nature by Faith: Studies in Reformation Theology in an Era of Global Emergency. Eugene, OR: Cascade Books, 2020.
EcoActivist Testament: Explorations of Faith and Nature for Fellow Travelers. Eugene, OR: Cascade Books, 2022.

www.ingramcontent.com/pod-product-compliance
Lightning Source LLC
Chambersburg PA
CBHW020854160426
43192CB00007B/918